Free to Be Yourself

JERRY SAVELLE

Free to Be Yourself

ISBN 0-9702911-5-9
Unless otherwise stated, all Scripture
quotations are taken from
The King James Version of the Bible.

Jerry Savelle Ministries International
P.O. Box 748
Crowley, TX 76036
(817) 297-3155
www.jsmi.org

Table of Contents

Are You Comfortable With Yourself?

1

Chapter One

It's hard to be free to be yourself when you're *not exactly* sure who you are. It's even harder if you know who you are but don't like yourself. You have been given specific physical features, personality traits, talents, and even hobbies that are all unique to your God-given purpose and assignment on this earth. Nothing about you is by accident. Even the challenges you've had to overcome throughout your life serve a purpose today. Your past experiences are all a part of the message of hope God has given you to share with others. When you discover how all of these features come together for one overall assignment on your life, you'll finally, confidently be free to be yourself!

> *To be yourself in a world that is constantly trying to make you something else is the greatest accomplishment.*
> *– Ralph Waldo Emerson*

Every challenge you've had to overcome should serve as an encouragement to someone else. Every battle you've faced, every temptation you've overcome, and every victory you've enjoyed are all part of your life story for others to read, hear about, or learn from. You just have to see it that way.

I don't know of one single person who just absolutely loves everything about themselves. We all have areas we wish we could change whether it's in our appearance or our personality or our abilities. The focus of this book is to help you realize who you are, how God sees you, how you see yourself, and how others see you. In doing so, you will stop focusing on your weaknesses and comparing yourself with others, and instead learn to draw out and appreciate your individual strengths and begin to run with them.

My purpose is to help you realize how uniquely you were made and how to turn all those things you don't like about yourself into strengths that set you apart from everyone else. The very thing that you always thought was your worst attribute or *quirk* could be the very thing that attracts people to want to know more about you and the God you serve.

In fact, you ought to be a trendsetter instead of a trend-follower. You ought to be setting the pattern for the world to follow, instead of the other way around. The Bible tells us to adorn the Gospel of Jesus Christ (Titus 2:10) to make it attractive, beautiful, and appealing, so it will draw people.

Believers ought to be fashionable. God doesn't want us looking like a bunch of refugees from the city dump while the rest of the world is keeping up with the times. The world ought to be looking to us Christians to set the standard. They should be watching us, how we dress and conduct ourselves. The world should be taking its cue from us, not vice versa. But that can't happen without a truthful realization of exactly who you are and what you were created to do. It comes from being the original that you already are and not a copy of someone else and being comfortable with yourself.

When you gain confidence in who you are in Christ Jesus, in the love He has for you, and the special uniqueness He's given you, you'll be free to be your own trendsetter.

And be not conformed to this world: but be ye transformed by the renewing of your mind, that ye may prove what is that good, and acceptable, and perfect, will of God.

Romans 12:2

If you've become stifled into a box of what every Christian is "supposed" to be like or look like or act like, it's time to break out and be yourself. The very qualities, talents, and even hobbies that God has put in you, could be the very thing that attracts others to Jesus.

Being comfortable with who you are

Whatever it is that you believe God has called you to do, whether it is full-time ministry, business, politics, the sports arena, whatever it is, God wants you to succeed at it.

The primary reason is so that He will look good! Your success will make the God you serve attractive. That is what it is all about. It is not about you *preaching,* but it is about you living God's principles that produce success, and eventually someone is going to want to know how you did it. When you can tell them that Jesus is Lord of your life and God is your source, it makes the God you serve very attractive.

Before I formed thee in the belly I knew thee . . .

Jeremiah 1:5 (Amplified)

It is interesting that God has known you for a long, long time. If there is anybody who knows you, knows what you are like, and what makes you tick, so to speak, it is God. He knew you before you were ever formed in your mother's womb.

Before I formed you in the womb I knew [and] approved of you . . .
Jeremiah 1:5 (Amplified)

Do you feel unique?

Have you ever been told that you are unique? Many people feel they have nothing special to offer, nothing rare about them, they just sort of blend in with the crowd. I want to prove to you that you are different, uncommon, and so unique to anyone else in this entire world. **Unique** means *only one of its kind, exceptional, distinctive, matchless, irreplaceable, and rare.*

Do you feel that way when you look in the mirror or when you walk into a large auditorium filled with people? Do you "stand out" as being the only one of a kind? If that's not your perception of yourself . . . it should be. Why? Because according to medical science, you are the only one in this entire world with your fingerprints. Nobody else's matches yours. You are the only person with the DNA that you have. Not one person around the globe can match your hair follicles and dental impressions. Out of 7 billion people, not one! Only you have what you have.

Just as we've been told that no two zebras have the same stripe pattern, there is no other person uniquely formed and created the way God created ***you.***

The problem with most people is that although we are each uniquely made, we never take the time to discover our uniqueness or we overlook our creative selves as no big deal, nothing special, *surely God can't use that!*

Later in the book we are going to actually take a look into your personality, discovering your strengths, weaknesses, and unique personality type, which I believe will give you an understanding of who you are and how you relate to the world around you.

Before we get there, it's vitally important that you realize your uniqueness in God by understanding who you are in His eyes first. If you don't ever gain this foundation, you cannot build any further. It's like building the framework of a house without setting the concrete foundation. The house will fall.

You must accept that God loves you right where you are, your past and all . . . if you're ever going to be what He created you to be. I understand it's challenging to comprehend such a love and it's only human nature to try to earn it. But trust me, there's nothing you or I could ever do to earn what Jesus did. That's why it only comes by making an active, deliberate choice to simply receive it for yourself. Take it personally. In fact, it should make you that much more thankful in your daily fellowship with God because we know we don't deserve His love. Receiving His love for you is step one.

Turning toys into tools

Automobiles, motorcycles, hot rods, fast cars, and classic automobiles were my life. I grew up loving cars and motorcycles. My Dad rode motorcycles. The first one I remember him having was a 1957 Harley. He put me on the back of that bike and Harley Davidson's got in my blood! Dad raced automobiles. He raced everything – modified hot rods, sport cars, you name it. The only thing he didn't race was dragsters. I was the one who got into that when I got old enough. Dad always said, "I don't mind you racing, son. Just do it legal." But it was more fun in the streets of Shreveport, Louisiana.

So I grew up around cars and motorcycles. I grew up with a passion for that. There are people who like cars and motorcycles, and then there are people who love it. Do you know what I am talking about? It's the same with musicians. There are people who wish they could play a guitar. Then there are other people who ***are part*** of the guitar. It is part of their personality. I mean they eat, sleep, and drink it. They get excited going into a music store. They see all those guitars lined up and they start getting hyper. I don't understand it, but boy when I walk into a motorcycle shop, it is the same thing; that same adrenaline.

I don't think those things are by accident. I don't think it is a coincidence. I think it is something God put in us. Why would a guy be born with, or at least as far back as he can remember, an immediate love and passion for cars and motorcycles? There has got to be a reason for that.

Well, in 1969, I gave all that up when I went into the ministry. I wanted to show God that He was number one in my life. I got rid of all of my hot rods. I owned a paint and body restoration shop, and I got out of that. I had three classic cars that I was working on at the time and I got rid of those. I quit riding motorcycles. I wanted to show God that He was number one and that I was willing to let go of all of that to serve Him. For the next ten years, I never picked up a hot rod magazine. I never went to a race. I never rode a motorcycle. I just walked away from it totally.

I really did not think at the time that a preacher was *allowed* to have anything like that. I didn't know any preacher at the time who rode motorcycles. I didn't know any preachers who went to the drag races. I didn't know any preachers who had fast automobiles. So, I walked away from it all.

Then about ten years later, God started giving it back to me. I questioned Him about it. I asked, "Why are you doing this? I didn't ask for this. I gave all that up for You."

He said, "Number one – *now I know I can trust you with it. I know I am first place in your life and not some car or motorcycle."* Then He said, *"Secondly, I know this will bring joy to your life, and if it brings joy to you, it will bring joy to Me." "Thirdly,"* He said, ***"Turn your toys into tools*** *and use them for My sake. Turn them into evangelistic tools. Use them for the Gospel."*

I have preached for thirty-six years now and most people see me in a suit all the time. They see me in a convention center or in a conference or in a church and yes, that is a part of me, but it is not all of me. It is not what I am really all about. Even though preaching is my life, I still have a passion for cars and bikes.

Now for someone to try to take that away from me because they don't think it's the way a Christian should be or a preacher should be, would suppress something God wants to use. God has already said, "I knew you before I formed you and I approved of you." So, God can actually use what once was a "toy" in my life as a "tool" to win the lost. It wasn't a coincidence that I enjoyed those things. I know it makes me a little different, but you have got to become comfortable with who you are; be comfortable with being different from the average person.

Like many people today, the Prophet Jeremiah was having an identity problem. God had chosen him to do a certain task, but Jeremiah kept saying, "I can't do this. I am inadequate. I don't feel like I can do what You are asking me to do."

He told God in Jeremiah 1:6 – . . . *Lord God! Behold, I cannot speak: for I am a child.*

But listen to what God says, . . . *Say not, I am a child: for thou shalt go to all that I shall send thee, and whatsoever I command thee thou shalt speak. Be not afraid of their faces: for I am with thee . . .*

Every time Jeremiah said, *"I can't,"* God said, "You can." *But you don't understand . . .* God says, *"It is you who doesn't understand. I made you and I approve of you and I not only believe that you can do this but I will equip you to do it"* (Author's paraphrase).

Notice that God is telling Jeremiah, "If you will see yourself the way I see you . . . then you will be able to conquer your fears. You will overcome your low self-esteem and you will succeed in what I have called you to do . . . in your own unique way."

So many people today, including Christians, have low self-esteem. They don't like who they are and they are always wishing they could be like somebody else. Well, it is not going to happen. You are not going to be somebody else. You can buy a guitar and go through the motions but that does not make you a musician.

Many people lack proper self-esteem, they imitate someone else, and as a result, life can be painful and tremendously difficult. You need proper self-esteem, not high-mindedness or arrogance, but self-esteem that is founded on the Word of God based on how God sees you. It is vital to your success in life. God made you and He wants you to be comfortable with who you are.

Did you notice in the Amplified version God said to Jeremiah, *"I approve of you."* That means you are okay as far as God is concerned. He likes you just like you are. Yes, we are constantly making adjustments in our lives. There are certain things from time to time that the Spirit of God may deal with us about that will improve our lives and make us better. All of us have character flaws that we need to work on, but what I am talking about is God really likes you. If I ignored my passion for cars and motorcycles because I feel "different" than most preachers, I would not be my true self. You have to become comfortable with who you are . . . <u>all</u> of you. If you enjoy decorating or fishing or hunting or making crafts, enjoy it. Don't suppress things because you feel different or you don't think God can do anything with it. He can.

I hated being short!

Growing up, I was so shy and bashful. When my mother left me at school that first day, I cried and cried and cried. The teacher called my mother and said, "This boy is really shy." I will never forget her. Her name was Miss Pearson. Miss Pearson was such a sweetheart. She really worked with me. She helped me fit into the crowd, but I was still bashful at the end of first grade. She was so concerned about me that she went to the principal and said, "I want to go to second grade so I can be with Jerry," and she was my second grade teacher as well.

When I got a little older, I found out that I was *little* and that bothered me. I was short for my age. Even the girls were bigger than me. I was always self-conscious about my size because I was so small, skinny, and short. In the sixth grade, our class had a play and they chose me to do the lead part. Well, I had gotten over some of my bashfulness and shyness, so I was brave enough to be in the school play. But the girl who was doing the lead female part was even taller than the teacher! She was a big girl. I looked up at her all the time. At the end of the play, I rescued the leading lady and in the very last scene, she was supposed to thank me and say; "Oh my hero," but instead of just leaning down and saying, "Oh thank you, you are my hero," she picked me up and kissed me on the cheek (my feet were just dangling) and then she put me back down. I was so embarrassed.

My parents moved a lot when I was young. I went through about three or four different elementary schools. Before the first day was up at each school, I was called "Little Jerry" because there was always a "normal" Jerry. So in order to separate the two of us, he was "Jerry" and I was "Little Jerry." The teacher even called me that. If I would raise my hand, she would say, "What is it, Little Jerry?" I hated it. I hated being little.

I wanted to be big. I wanted to play football. Do you think they would let me play football? No. They were always concerned I would get hurt. I had friends who were big and muscular and just naturally built and they would not play football. I would say, "You make me so mad. You are big. You are muscular. You have natural talent and you won't even go out for football. I wish I had your body."

The tragedy of life is not that it ends so soon, but that we wait so long to begin it.
– Unknown

There is always something that somebody dislikes about themselves. Take for instance, that person who is extremely tall. The tall person wishes they were shorter. The skinny person wishes they were heavier. The fat person wishes they were skinnier.

Don't misunderstand me, I am not talking about self-improvement. There is always room for us to improve ourselves. There is always room for discipline and those kinds of things, but what I am talking about is when you are constantly down on yourself. When you have low self-esteem and you are always comparing yourself to someone else or you're always wishing you were someone else. If you continue to do this, then you will never enjoy the life that God plans for you to enjoy.

You will never experience a very high level of success if you are constantly down on yourself. You have got to remember that God approves of you.

But by the grace of God I am what I am . . .

I Corinthians 15:10

By the grace of God, I am what I am and by the grace of God, you are what you are. Be grateful for who you are. The world would be a dull place if every one of us were exactly alike. If every one of us had exactly the same personality, same opinions, same ideas, same ideals, the world would be very boring. That is the reason God made you unique. You are special to God. There is something about you that no one else can quite duplicate.

There are impersonators who can act like, look like, and even talk like celebrities. They impersonate someone and can be very convincing, but it's just an *impersonation.* It's not the real them. Many times, there are Christians who come into church every Sunday with a mask on and it is not the real them.

By constantly rejecting who you are, you limit your ability to succeed. You will find yourself shunning other people because you don't think you are as good as them. You will shy away from taking risks, particularly when it comes to your career for fear of rejection or fear of failure. You will endeavor to build walls of defense so that no one can see the you that you see all the time. You will constantly make excuses as to why success seems to have escaped ***you.***

Some people turn to drugs and alcohol because of their low self-esteem and their rejection of who they are. The real answer is discovering how God sees you. And then determine that is the way you are going to see yourself from now on. Determine that no matter what anybody else says or anybody else thinks, you are going to see yourself the way God sees you. How you perceive yourself will have a drastic effect on how successful you will become.

You're not alone

One of the greatest revelations that you could ever receive is that God is with you. How many times have you seen that phrase in the Bible? It must be hundreds of times. ***"Fear not, I am with thee."*** Knowing that God is with you just gives you a boost. Whatever tasks you may face each day, you are not facing them alone.

The real battle you are facing is on the inside. Way down. Many people may not be able to see that you are going through a battle because you can put on a front. I know a lot of people, whom you would never suspect, that seem very bold outwardly; but they constantly battle depression. Their being bold and loud is just a way to hide it, but deep down inside they are tormented. In the crowd, they are loud. They are the center of attention and they always have something funny to say, and you think, "Boy, that is a cool guy." But when he leaves that crowd, goes home and is all alone, he is fighting depression. Why is that? He has not discovered who he is based on the way God sees him and he is uncomfortable being himself.

When you begin to see yourself the way God sees you, no matter what anybody else says and no matter what you may have been told all your life, your self-esteem will rise.

You may have had parents who just didn't know any better, and they put you down all the time and said cruel words about you.

"You will never be anything."

"You are so dumb."

"You are so stupid."

"You are just like your father."

Those words wound your spirit and you grow up not being able to express who you really are because you are afraid somebody might see what is going on inside. God wants you to be free to be you. He likes you. He thinks you are wonderful.

You can change how you feel about yourself if you will spend more time looking in the mirror of God's Word instead of looking in that mirror in your bathroom. You may not like what you see in the bathroom mirror but if you will look in the mirror of God's Word, you will eventually be changed into that same image. When you spend enough time in the Word of God, what it says will become more real to you than what you see in the natural. You will become what the Word says you are. You will be transformed into the image that God planned for you.

And all of us, as with unveiled face, [because we] continued to behold [in the Word of God] as in a mirror the glory of the Lord, are constantly being transfigured into his very own image in ever increasing splendor and from one degree of glory to another . . .

II Corinthians 3:18 (Amplified)

The more you look in the mirror of God's Word, the more you are going to be changed into that image. I am happy with being who I am today and obviously, I am not shy anymore. I am not timid. I am not afraid. It doesn't even bother me that I'm short. I like little Jerry now.

I am happy with who I am and what God is doing in my life. I don't want to be anybody else. I like what I am doing and I like the way God made me. And I want you to feel the same way about yourself. If God's Word can change my opinion of myself, it can change yours. Looking at yourself the way God sees you, enables you to make an accurate assessment of yourself. You won't become puffed up or arrogant but you will become confident in who you are. You will begin to recognize that you are unique and that there is no one else quite like you.

You are not a mistake

My frame was not hidden from You when I was being formed in secret [and] intricately and curiously wrought . . . Your eyes saw my unformed substance, and in your book all the days [of my life] were written before ever they took shape . . .

Psalm 139:15-16 (Amplified)

I don't care if you were born out of wedlock. You are not a mistake. God knew you before you were formed and He approved of you. Don't allow anybody to tell you that you are a mistake. It's time to start liking yourself. Get comfortable with who you are. Don't let anybody else try to make you what you are not. God made you. He likes you and He thinks that you are wonderful. He approves of you and He believes that He can use your personality. He can use your style. He can use your size, your looks, and your gifts for His glory.

If there are areas in your life where you know you've felt intimidated, inadequate, and insecure, then this book is going to build your self-esteem and dramatically improve your self-image so you can confidently be free to be yourself.

1

"I feel sorry for the guy who will marry you."

From mood swings to stability

Meet Laura . . .

If there was one thing I didn't like about myself it was that I was a moody person growing up. As I got older, my moods seemed to get worse. I would go from being angry and explosive to feeling depressed and sullen. As a teenager, there were times I would lock myself up in my room and stay for hours on end without speaking to anyone. Friends and family would tell me they felt sorry for the guy who was going to marry me because I was such a difficult person to be around. **These words would sting my heart,** every time someone would say them to me, but I knew they were right. I finally did fall in love with a wonderful guy and he was the one I wanted to marry and spend the rest of my life with.

It was time for me to change this part of my personality and I knew I couldn't do it on my own.

I prayed and asked the Lord to show me how and He did! I used a book of the Bible, Galatians 5:22-23, *But the fruit of the Spirit is love, joy, peace, longsuffering, gentleness, goodness, faith, meekness, temperance: against such there is no law.* The Lord also reminded me of the Broadway play song, "The King and I." In the lyrics it says, "make-believe you're brave and the trick will take you far, you may be as brave as you make believe you are."

I changed the words to the lyrics a little and put "make-believe you're not moody and the trick will take you far, you may not be as moody as you make-believe you are!" I would sing that to myself when I would feel a negative mood coming on. God was showing me how to not go by my feelings all the time. And, as for that wonderful guy I wanted to marry, we got married! I can't say he married a totally different person at that time, but **I was in the process of changing for the better.**

It wasn't until we had been married for a couple of years that a friend brought it to my attention how happy and balanced I seemed to be. That's when I realized how far I had come. God replaced my moodiness with joy and peace. My husband and I have been married for almost 22 years and when I'm being a bit feisty, he'll tease me and say, "your family warned me about marrying you" and we'll both laugh and he'll say "you've come a long way baby"!

– Laura
Married with three children
Receptionist
41

Let's get started building by creating the **foundation**: how does God see you?

I remember trying to make a deal with God once. It proved to be such a traumatic experience, I never did it again.

When I was a teenage boy, I was involved in athletics and had a desire to be the greatest pole-vaulter in the world. I wanted to break the high school record, and even the world record. I had been practicing all summer and could hardly wait for track season to begin. Finally, it came around.

The day before it was to begin, I knelt down at my bed and prayed, "Lord, if You'll help me break the record, if You'll make me the greatest pole-vaulter in the world, I'll serve You."

The next day, the opening day of the new season, I was practicing my jumps when suddenly, out of nowhere, I fell and broke my left leg! That moment ended my chances of being "world champion" right then!

But the sad thing is that I thought it was *God* Who had done it to me because I had tried to make *a deal* with Him. So for a long time after that, I had a bad image of God. I would tell people, "Don't try to make any deals with God or He'll break your leg!"

Another time, one Sunday morning, I didn't go to church because I had decided to stay home and work on my car. I had it jacked up and was underneath it pulling the transmission, when it suddenly fell off the stands. I just knew that I was going to be crushed to death, but I wasn't.

Instead of thanking God for saving my life, I blamed Him for the accident. I figured He was mad at me for not going to church. *He had only broken my leg the first time* I reasoned, now He was determined to "do me in." Needless to say, I had a very poor concept of God and His ways. I didn't know how much He really loved me.

Your self-image should, first and foremost, be determined by how God sees you. So, let's find out straight from His mouth so there's no room for arguments or disputes. Let's allow the Word of God to be final authority and let's discover His opinion of how He sees you. But first, let's see exactly what you think about Him.

What do <u>you</u> think about God?

Many people today have the same misconception of God that I had. They think He is "out to get them" for their sins. Or they think if they don't serve Him, they will "suffer" for it. Therefore, their servitude is not motivated by love, but by fear.

Then there are those who serve God only because of what they think He will do for them. We cannot serve God out of a sense of fear or out of selfish motives. We must serve God because we love Him. We must serve God, not from a sense of obligation or duty, but from a sense of love. We must do it because He loves us, and because we love Him.

Contrary to what I thought about God growing up, I have come to realize that we are so special to God that He thinks about us all the time. In fact, as far as He is concerned, there is not another person on this planet who can take your place. When God thinks about you, a smile comes on His face.

Sometimes *our* love is conditional. It is based on what others will do for us. "I love You if..." God doesn't love us *if,* He loves us *regardless.* True love, real love, is always unconditional. That's why our love for Him should not be based upon what He will do for us. He wants us to love Him as He loves us, *regardless.*

The reason we are conditional about our love for God is because we are conditional about our love for each other: "I love you, if you agree with me ... or behave like I want you to ... comply with my standards or come up to my expectations."

We tend to express our love in proportion to the degree we think the other person "deserves" it. We naturally assume that God is as conditional with His love as we are with ours.

You might be thinking, "Oh, but Jerry, you don't realize what I've done in my life." It doesn't matter. God believes in what happened at Calvary even if no one else does. When God looks at you, He looks through the Blood of Jesus and sees someone whom He loves very much, and He has great plans for your life!

God wants to do some BIG things in your life, but they will only happen in direct proportion to your ability to comprehend His great love for you. That is the foundation upon which everything else is built. If you don't believe God loves you, then you won't believe He created you for a unique purpose on earth. You must get this settled in your life. To *comprehend* means: *to grasp, to catch hold of, to seize, to take in, and to completely understand.*

People who are unable to comprehend the love of God are limited as to how much they can receive from God. Can you truly say that you have a strong grip on how much God really loves you? Has your heart truly taken it in to the point that you are totally convinced?

Someone once said, "God loved us the way we were, but He loves us too much to leave us that way." If you have truly comprehended this love, then you can no longer call yourself "worthless" or "a nobody." His love has made you the righteousness of God.

. . . but I don't deserve His love

You are somebody special to Him! It's not because of what you've done, but because of what Jesus did. Take it in, lay hold of it, seize this revelation. The larger it becomes on the inside of you, the more you'll enjoy God's best for your life.

You may be saying, "But I don't deserve this unconditional love. You don't know the horrible things I've done." Does anyone on this planet "deserve" what Jesus did? Absolutely not! You CANNOT earn God's love, you simply have to receive it.

. . . I thank thee that ***thou hast heard me.*** *And I knew that thou hearest me always . . .*

John 11:41-42

True comprehension of God's love causes you to know that He always hears you. You might say, "But that was Jesus." Yes, but listen to what He prayed for you and me.

. . . hast loved them, as thou hast loved me.

John 17:23

God loves you and me just as much as He loves Jesus. Can you comprehend that?

The more you comprehend, the more of God's fullness you will experience. The more you comprehend, the more convinced you will become of your unlimited possibilities.

The Lord is gracious, and full of compassion; slow to anger, and of great mercy. The Lord is good to all . . .

Psalm 145:8-9

Full of compassion means: *to love tenderly, to be full of eager yearning.* "The Lord is gracious" literally means: He is disposed to show favor.

Can you comprehend God's favor coming upon you to the point that your life is blessed a thousand times more than it is right now? Before you answer, rebuke the temptation to say, "I can't imagine that." That could be your very problem!

This is why we've been so limited. We "can't imagine" because we haven't truly comprehended His love toward us. Comprehended love declares: "If God said it, that settles it and I can have it!"

I want you to know that you haven't seen your best days yet. They are not behind you – they are ahead of you. You have so much to look forward to in your life, but you must, once and for all, believe **with no doubts** that God loves you!

God is no respecter of persons. He's not. He loves us all equally! He will bless anyone who will allow Him to do so.

You were always on His mind

The Lord hath been mindful of us: he will bless us . . .

Psalm 115:12

Look what's on the mind of God – you. God sits on His throne thinking of how He can bless you. And the Bible says that He never sleeps nor slumbers, so while you're sleeping, He's thinking up more ways to bless you when you awake.

He said, "I'll bless you coming in, I'll bless you going out. I'll bless you in the city, and I'll bless you in the field . . ." God's got blessings chasing us down everywhere we go. If you say, "Well, my life's not like that." It could be because of your lack of understanding of the Father's love.

One of the greatest joys that my wife Carolyn and I share is to see this work in our children. They've never been taught that miracles have passed away. All they know is that God is good! They have watched God do the miraculous in this family time and time again. They have never seen God disappoint this family. They have witnessed God's restoration in our lives. And now that they are adults and have children of their own, it is a joy to see God doing the same things for them that He's done for us!

We've taught them that God's not against them, He is for them, but we've also taught them that you must put Him first! Receive His love *with no strings* attached and then just love Him back.

So what is on the mind of God? You. Even when you disappoint Him, He still loves you. Even when you fall short, He still loves you. Why? Because He **is** love. He can't help Himself. Love is Who He is. He doesn't write you off when you make a mistake. He's the God of the second chance! And the third! And the fourth!

Before you go to sleep tonight, the devil would love to try to convince you that God may love others but not you. He's a liar. He knows what will happen once you finally accept and embrace God's love. You will be free to be yourself. And he doesn't like that!

Being confident of this very thing, that he which hath begun a good work in you will perform it until the day of Jesus Christ.

Philippians 1:6

. . . bring it to a flourishing finish . . .

Philippians 1:6 (The Message Translation)

You have a "flourishing finish" awaiting you!

God wants to turn every test in your life into a testimony! He wants to bless you no matter how impossible your situation may seem. In fact, He wants to bless you beyond your wildest dreams! He wants to restore every single thing Satan has stolen from you. God wants to see you free to be the wonderful, unique you that He created.

He wants you to discover your strengths, embrace your uniqueness, and recognize your hobbies and interests as something He Himself put into you and wants to use. But it all starts with knowing He loves you.

Does anyone care?

Knowing that there is somebody out there who loves you makes you feel good inside. But how often have you felt unloved and felt as though there is absolutely no one out there who even cares about you? Those are the lies of the Devil; don't listen to them. Listen to what the Word of God says:

The Lord make his face shine upon thee, and be gracious unto thee: The Lord lift up his countenance upon thee, and give thee peace.

Numbers 6:25-26

What is He saying? You are the object of God's affection. If you were the only human being alive on the planet, God would have sent Jesus to die for you. That's how much you're loved by the Father. I believe you are going to experience a real deliverance simply because you've realized you're loved and highly favored of God. He cares about you. He cares about every detail of your life. **He cares.**

Right this minute, if you read that last statement and didn't take it personally then you are believing the lies of Satan. He is a LIAR! You have to actively say with your mouth, "Lord, I believe You love me. I believe You have forgiven me. I believe You care. Thank You for loving me." Say that over and over and over again until finally, you'll begin to believe it more than you do Satan's lies!

What shall we then say to these things? If God be for us, who can be against us? He that spared not his own Son, but delivered him up for us all, how shall he not with him also freely give us all things?

Romans 8:31-32

There are a lot of people who are not convinced that God's for them. They think God's the enemy. How would you like to be commander-in-chief of an army where half of your troops don't even know who the enemy is? They've got their weapons pointed toward headquarters, blaming you all the time for their problems!

There are people questioning God, "Why did You let this happen to me?" They don't realize that God is for them and not against them! God did not cause this awful situation in your life to prove something to you; He cares about you. You are so loved by God that He is willing to give you freely ALL things. He's on your side!

Who is he that condemneth? It is Christ that died . . .

Romans 8:34

You shouldn't be living in condemnation. You shouldn't be listening to the lies of the Devil condemning you all the time and telling you how lousy you are, what a failure and a nobody you are. A person who listens to that all the time does not have a revelation of the love, honor, and favor of God.

You're so highly favored of the Lord that He says *no weapon formed against you shall prosper . . .* (Isaiah 54:17). You've been justified in the sight of God, not because of what you've done – because of what Jesus did FOR

YOU! NOTHING can separate you from God's love! Nothing, nothing, absolutely nothing!

For I am persuaded, that neither death, nor life, nor angels, nor principalities, nor powers, nor things present, nor things to come, nor height, nor depth, nor any other creature, shall be able to separate us from the love of God, which is in Christ Jesus our Lord.

Romans 8:38-39

When you become "persuaded" of just how loved you are, and just how valuable you are in the sight of God, then you can say what Paul said, "there is **nothing** that can separate me from the love of Christ. Not things present nor things to come."

You are somebody special. Quit running yourself down. Quit talking ugly about yourself. Quit talking about what a failure you are. Don't talk about how unworthy you are. You are the handiwork of God. You are loved. You are highly favored of God.

Clearing things up

It's one thing *never* to have heard the Truth, but then it's something else to have heard wrong information. There are many people who have heard wrong things about Jesus, and that's why they have never accepted Him.

There are two kinds of unbelief. One is caused by a **lack of knowledge;** the other is a result of an **unwillingness to believe.** One person does not believe simply because he doesn't know anything. Because of a lack of knowledge concerning that particular subject, he can't believe. Another person has heard the truth but, as an act of his own will, has decided not to believe. There are many people who have decided not to believe in Jesus because of all the wrong things they have heard about Him.

Many times that distorted image has come from Christians. They see God as some kind of vicious tyrant who is just looking for an opportunity to "bust them over the head" the first time they do something wrong. The idea that all I have to look forward to is God knocking me out every time I make a mistake would keep me from wanting to become one of His children, too.

God is a God of love, mercy, compassion, kindness, and goodness; but how can you experience that if you don't believe it and receive it for **yourself?**

Probably the most famous scripture in the Bible is all about . . . you guessed it . . . God's amazing love for us.

For God so loved the world, that he gave his only begotten Son, that whosoever believeth in him should not perish, but have everlasting life.

John 3:16

You have right-standing with the God of the universe, and your right-standing with God gives you the ability to stand in His presence without a sense of sin, guilt, fear, inferiority, or condemnation. You have just as much right to stand before God as Jesus does. He purchased that right for you. You are enjoying His righteousness! Or you should be! Start dwelling on these things and allow them to become a reality in your inner man.

When this becomes a reality in your spirit, you will quote I John 4:4 with an assurance you have never known before. GREATER IS HE THAT IS IN ME, THAN HE THAT IS IN THE WORLD.

I encourage you to confess daily, "Thank you, Lord, for loving me. I receive your love by faith in Jesus' Name!" Continue to say it until you are convinced of His love. It will change everything. If you still don't have it engrained in you and you're still struggling with God actually forgiving you and loving you, then you need to take a moment and read this chapter again. Read the scriptures out loud. It must be the foundation before we can build any further.

Who are you really?

People all over the world have asked the question, "Who am I?" Many people have lost sight of who they are, simply because of what others have told them. Many have been told they are a failure, they're nobodies, they're useless, and many other hurtful words.

Your circumstances do not determine who you are. Your financial situation doesn't determine who you are. Your appearance doesn't even determine who you are. Today, you're going to find out exactly who you are!

If you don't know who you are, then you will live beneath your privileges as a child of God. If you don't know who you are, you will never enjoy God's best for your life.

I'm not talking about who you were born to in the natural. I'm not talking about your natural father and mother. I'm talking about who you are in Christ Jesus. Keeping you from finding out who you are is one of the major tactics of the enemy. That's how he keeps you in bondage.

Most people in the world today feel rejected. They've been told things all of their lives that have kept them down and held them back. You may be one of these people that have been held back or oppressed because of what you've been told. You may have been told that God didn't love you. You may have been told that you will never amount to anything. You may have been born in poverty and told that you will always be poor! But if you go to the Bible, you will find out **that's not what God says!** In fact, if you get God in your life, He will elevate things around you. He will bless you beyond your wildest dreams. God will take you in His arms and He will clothe you with His Word. Then He will hold you up to the world like a trophy and He will say to the world, "See what My Word can do!"

Big on the inside

As I mentioned before, when I was a young boy, I was very small for my age. I hated being "Little Jerry" because when you're little, people think you're weak. They think you're frail. They think you can't do what the bigger boys can do. And when you're little, there's always someone bigger who likes to bully you so he can prove how big he is. So when you're little, you have to learn to fight. I was always little and the big guys always picked on me.

Sometimes I would go home crying because they would push me around. My Father said to me one day, "Tonight, you're going to learn how to protect yourself."

I said, "Dad, you don't understand. The boys in my school are much bigger than me! I can't even reach them!"

He said, "Then hit them in their legs!"

So he taught me how to box. Every night, when he would come home from work, we had a boxing lesson. My Mother didn't like this, but my Father said, "This boy will never run from another fight!"

There was this big bully in my class. He was my age but he was twice my size! He was almost as big as the teacher. He talked big! He pushed people around! He threatened everybody! He took things from others and wouldn't give them back. Then he dared them to fight him! Everybody was afraid of him. When you saw him, you hoped he didn't see you because if he saw you, he would push you and take things from you.

One day, he took something that belonged to me. It was something my Father had given me, and it was very special to me. He would not give it back. He put it in his pocket and walked away. I said, "Give it back!" He said, "Make me, Little Jerry!" He challenged me, and the other boys heard it and gathered around. They were about to see him **"kill"** Little Jerry. They could hardly wait! So I'm standing there in that circle, and all these boys were watching us.

He said, "Make me give it back, Little Jerry," and he pushed me and I fell down.

I wanted to cry, but I didn't. Instead, I got back up and said, "Give it to me!"

He said, "Make me!" and he pushed me and I fell down again.

I got up one more time and I said, "I'm not running from you today! If you don't give it to me, you and me are going to fight!"

He said, "You're going to fight me? You can't even reach me, Little Jerry!"

So he turned around to say something to the other boys, and while he wasn't looking, I made a fist. When he turned back around, I jumped up and hit him in the nose! Blood was pouring. He fell down flat on his back! No one could believe it! I couldn't even believe it! He was crying! He was bleeding! So I thought, *This is my opportunity.* So I jumped on his chest and punched him again until he begged me to leave him alone!

I said, "Give me what belongs to me!"

He said, "I will if you stop hitting me!"

I said, "Give it to me or I'll hit you again."

He gave it to me and he never took anything from me again. The older we got, the bigger he got. He remained a bully but he never bothered me again. In fact, when he saw me coming, he would walk the other way. Well, Satan is a bully! He talks big. He says, "You're nothing. You have nothing to offer the world and you never will." And you'll eventually believe him if you don't know who you are in Christ Jesus. But you are more than a conqueror! You are unique. When you find out who you are in Christ, Satan will start running the other way. What matters is how big your God is on the inside of you.

Who does God think you are?

Discovering who you are changes everything. In Exodus chapter 3, we find the story of God appearing unto Moses out of a burning bush.

God called unto him and said, "Moses, Moses." And he said, "Here am I."
Exodus 3:4

God begins to talk to Moses and tells him that He has heard the cry of His people. His people had been afflicted and oppressed. They began to cry for deliverance, and God was about to raise up a Deliverer. God cares about afflicted people. God has a heart for people who are oppressed. It's not His will that you live in bondage, that you be afflicted, and oppressed. That is not God's best for your life.

He began to speak to Moses and He said, "I want to use you as a deliverer." Notice what Moses said:

*...**Who am I,** that I should go unto Pharaoh, and that I should bring forth the children of Israel out of Egypt?*

Exodus 3:11

Moses said, "Who am I?"

Moses asked a question that has been asked down through the ages. "Who am I?"

Well, by the time you finish reading this book, you're going to know exactly who you are. Who you truly are is not what man thinks. It's not what your relatives think. It's not what society thinks. It's not what you think when you look in the mirror. It's what God thinks that matters. And when you know who you are in Christ, then it changes your outlook on life. It changes your attitude. It changes your self-image, self-esteem, and potential. You begin to think like a winner and not a loser.

I want you to discover your identity in Christ. By stopping you from finding out your true identity, Satan can limit you. When you don't know who you are, Satan controls your mind. When you don't know who you are, Satan controls your finances. When you don't know who you are, Satan controls your destiny!

My people are destroyed for lack of knowledge . . .

Hosea 4:6

There is an abundance of knowledge in the Bible from Genesis to Revelation. In the Bible you will find out who you are – your true identity. And once you find it out, you will never be the same again! Your days of defeat will be over! Satan will no longer be your master! You will dominate him!

Don't believe what I'm telling you just because I say it. I encourage you to go to the Bible. Find out if what I'm saying is true. Don't take anyone's word for it. Find out what the Bible says for yourself. The Bible is true. God is not a man that He should lie. You owe it to yourself to go to the Bible and study it until it becomes your revelation and not just something you heard Jerry Savelle say!

You are what God says you are!

I once was a man without knowledge. I did not know who I was in Christ, and because of it, I lived a defeated life. I didn't know what God had done for me through the redemptive work of Jesus at Calvary. I thought I was just an average guy, working an average job, and living an average life. I didn't know that He had made me the righteousness of God. I didn't know that He had given me authority over the devil. I didn't know I was redeemed from sickness and disease. When you don't know these things, then you live in slavery to the adversary.

I thought I was a failure . . . failing in business, failing in my marriage, failing in my finances, nothing special about me . . . just existing day-to-day. But once I found out who I was in Christ Jesus, then something began to happen on the inside. There is a power called faith that rises up within you, and it causes you to believe that you are what God says you are! You begin to believe that you can do what God says you can do and you can have what God says you can have! You also begin to see that God gave you your personality on purpose. He may have given you an outgoing personality or maybe you're gentle and quiet. Maybe you're highly organized and have a plan for everything, or on the other hand, you're very spontaneous! God gave you unique traits to use . . . not dread.

I found this out over thirty-six years ago, and I have lived a victorious Christian life ever since. Satan is not my master. He does not control my destiny. I am in charge because I found out who I am. I am unique. And so are you.

"Religion" won't set you free

God has supplied an abundance of knowledge, but through religious tradition, Satan has kept the body of Christ in darkness. Religious tradition blinds the hearts and minds of God's people.

In II Corinthians 4:3, the apostle Paul tells us that . . . *if our gospel be hid, it is hid to them that are lost.* Satan wants to put blinders over your eyes so that you cannot see. That's what religious tradition does. Jesus said that religious tradition makes the Word of God of no affect in one's life.

It's not religious tradition that will set you free. It's not religious tradition that will heal your body. It's not religious tradition that will set your family free. *It's the truth!* And Jesus said, *"My Word is Truth."* The definition of the word ***truth*** is the *highest form of reality that exists.* The Bible is the highest form of reality that exists, and if you know the truth, Jesus said it will make you free!

The more truth you know, the more freedom you will enjoy. I'm a free man. I live in freedom because *I know the truth and the truth has made me free!*

You, too, can know the truth. It's not hidden **from** you. It's hidden **for** you! God has put His truth between Genesis and Revelation, and if you are hungry enough for freedom, then you'll get in God's Word. And if you continue in that Word, you will be free.

. . . If ye ***continue*** *in my Word, then are ye my disciples indeed; And ye shall know the truth, and the truth shall make you free.*

John 8:31-32

The only thing that can break the chains of bondage is truth. Are you ready to know the truth?

Out with the old

Therefore if any man be in Christ, he is a new creature: old things are passed away; behold, all things are become new.

II Corinthians 5:17

Once you come to Jesus – once you make Him Lord of your life, then you become a new creation. Your past is forgiven. The literal Greek tells us that you are *a new species of being that never existed before.*

Just like Saul of Tarsus on the road to Damascus – when he met Jesus, his life was changed forever. He became a new creation. Saul died and a new man began to live.

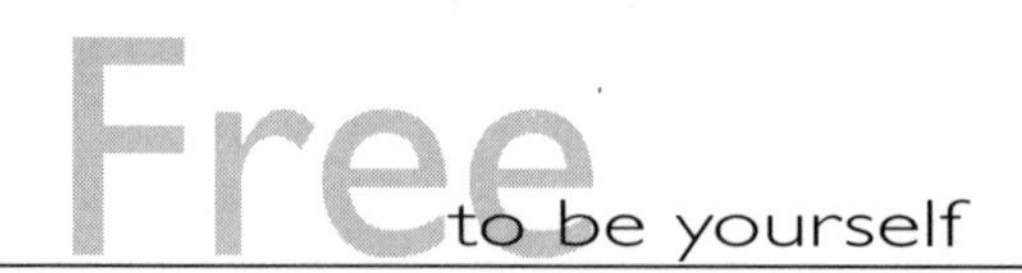

On February 11, 1969, at three o'clock in the morning, the old Jerry Savelle died when I met Jesus and a new Jerry Savelle came into existence. I'm not the same man. I don't think like that man. I don't talk like that man. That man is dead. I'm a new man! The old man lived in defeat. The new man lives in victory! Aren't you glad that Jesus has made you brand new?

You've been justified

For he hath made him to be sin for us, who knew no sin; that we might be made the ***righteousness of God in him.***

II Corinthians 5:21

As I mentioned before, you are the righteousness of God. Jesus died in your place. He took your sin and He made you righteous with His righteousness.

I know religious tradition says, "There's none righteous – no not one." That was before Jesus went to the cross. When He went to the cross, when He died and was raised from the dead, the Bible says, *"We were justified."* You were a sinner, but you were saved by grace and now you are the righteousness of God.

If you're going to live a life of victory, then you must have a revelation of the fact that you are the righteousness of God. You're not righteous because of what you've done. You're righteous because of what Jesus did.

God hears your prayers

The eyes of the Lord are upon the righteous, and His ears ***are open unto their cry.***

Psalm 34:15

The effectual fervent prayer of a righteous man availeth much.

James 5:16

. . . makes tremendous power available [dynamic in its working].

James 5:16 (Amplified)

That's what happens to a righteous man when he prays. And you are that righteous man or woman! God's eyes are over you and His ears are open to **your** prayers. When you pray, heaven stands at attention. When you pray, all the angels are on alert. When you pray, God says, "That's one of Mine. Let's answer their prayer!"

You now have the right to stand in God's presence as though sin has never occurred. You can stand in the presence of God without a sense of fear, guilt, or inferiority. You can stand in the presence of God because you are righteous. Jesus made you righteous, and there's nothing Satan can do about it!

You are a joint-heir with Jesus

The Spirit itself beareth witness with our spirit, that we are the children of God: And if children, then heirs; heirs of God, and joint-heirs with Christ; if so be that we suffer with him, that we may be also glorified together.

Romans 8:16-17

That simply means that God is **your** Father. You're an heir of God. You're a joint-heir with Jesus Christ. That means whatever Jesus gets, you get.

My earthly mother and father had two children. I'm the oldest and I have a sister who is four years younger. When my earthly father passed away and went to heaven, he left us an inheritance. My mother is still alive. I hope she stays alive until Jesus comes! But should she die before the appearing of the Lord, then my sister and I would inherit everything that my mother and father would leave. I'm an heir. My sister and I are joint-heirs. Everything they have – we get it – it's ours!

Now let me ask you a question. When do I get my inheritance? When my parents die or when I die? I get my inheritance when **my parents die** – not when I die. Some people think that they only get an inheritance from God when they die. No. You received your inheritance from God when Jesus died! Hallelujah!

You are an heir of God and a joint-heir with Jesus. Jesus is the only person who has ever lived and died and then was raised from the dead to see to it that His Will was carried out so that His joint-heirs get what is coming to them. Isn't that awesome? Doesn't it all make sense? You're a joint-heir with Jesus. That means you are entitled to healing. It's your inheritance. You're entitled to prosperity. It's your inheritance. You're entitled to victory and success. It's your inheritance. Don't wait until you get to heaven. You can have it now!

You are Abraham's seed

In Deuteronomy 28 the Bible tells us that if you belong to Christ, then you are Abraham's seed. You are an heir to the promise. You should read Deuteronomy 28 to find out what belongs to you. God promised Abraham that he would be blessed coming in, blessed going out, blessed in the city, blessed in the field, blessed in everything he set his hand to do. He would make him the head and not the tail – above and not beneath!

When his enemy comes in one way, God will cause him to flee seven ways. That's just a portion of the blessings of Abraham. And you are Abraham's seed! (Galatians 3:29).

You are more than a conqueror

Nay, in all these things we are more than conquerors through him that loved us.

Romans 8:37

No longer look at yourself as a loser. No longer say, "I never win." No longer say, "You don't understand my past." Quit saying, "You don't know my background." Quit saying, "You don't know where I was born!" These things make no difference if you are in Christ! If Jesus is Lord, then the Bible declares that YOU ARE MORE THAN A CONQUEROR!

When you have this revelation in your heart, then there can be no more defeat in your life! There can be no more bondage! You will not fail if you know that you are more than a conqueror.

You are a world overcomer

For whatsoever is born of God overcometh the world: and this is the victory that overcometh the world, even our faith.

I John 5:4

If you are born again, if you believe Jesus is Lord, if you believe you're born of God, then you are a world overcomer!

Many people today live in defeat because they do not understand the love of God. Some people think that God loves some more than others. Some people think that's the reason some are more blessed than others. Some think that God loves the white man more than the black man. This is not true. God is no respecter of persons. God loves each and every one of us the same. I'm no different from you. You are no different from me. What God's done in my life, He can do for you.

You are handpicked by God

According as he hath chosen us in him before the foundation of the world, that we should be holy and without blame before him in love.

Ephesians 1:4

The Bible says that God has chosen us before the foundation of the world. When you know you've been chosen, it makes you feel special.

Even as [in His love] He chose us ***[actually picked us out for Himself as His own]*** *in Christ before the foundation of the world, that we should be holy (consecrated and set apart for Him) and blameless in His sight, even above reproach, before Him in love.*

Ephesians 1:4 (Amplified)

The Apostle Paul used the word "elect." We are the elect of God. Do you know what that means? It means "handpicked by God." God handpicked each and everyone of us! You're special!

When you fully understand what Paul is saying, then it causes you to walk in your true identity. You begin to think, "Why wouldn't God bless me? Why wouldn't God heal me? Why wouldn't God give me victory? Why wouldn't God want to use me? I'm chosen by God. I'm handpicked by God. I've been set apart by God!" That should make you feel special and have great confidence that God is going to see you through, no matter what you're facing today. You are chosen by God. You are handpicked. You are set apart!

You are a special treasure

But ye are a chosen generation, a royal priesthood, an holy nation, ***a peculiar people;*** *that ye should show forth the praises of him who hath called you out of darkness into his marvellous light.*

I Peter 2:9

The Bible says we are a peculiar people. Do you know what this word means in the literal Greek? **Peculiar** means *special treasure.* What is God saying to us? He's saying that we are chosen, that we are handpicked, that we are set apart, and that we are His special treasure.

Don't ever let anyone tell you again that you are a nobody, that you are no good, or that you are not favored by God and that you have nothing special to offer the world. According to the Bible, you are a special treasure!

When you know these things, you can walk with your head up high, with a dance in your step, and with joy in your heart because you know that you know that you know that God is for you. And if God is for you, then no one can successfully be against you!

Fight for what is yours

Go to the Bible, study it, read it, pray over it, and ask God to reveal to you who you are in Christ Jesus. Once it becomes a revelation, no one can take it away from you. Satan cannot steal from you any longer. Tell him, "You've defeated me for the last time! You've held me back for the last time! I am the seed of Abraham, I am an heir of God, I am entitled to be blessed. I am entitled to health. I am entitled to prosperity! I am entitled to a wonderful future. You are not stealing it from me any longer."

You are a world overcomer. You are not a loser anymore! You are a winner in Christ Jesus!

You are going to find out, when you know who you are, and when you're absolutely convinced of God's love for you, that Satan will have to flee from you! Satan is a worthy opponent, but he is a defeated foe. Jesus has already defeated him. He has already stripped him of his authority and stripped him of his power! He cannot defeat you any longer.

This is the foundation to being free to be yourself, knowing that God loves and approves of you.

2

"I often wished I was more like the 'life of the party.'"

A quiet tongue earns respect

Meet Isaiah . . .

I have always been a quiet person. I tend to be more reflective and thoughtful while others seem to say everything that pops into their mind.

It is not as though I'm a shy person; I am simply less outgoing and talkative than others.

I have often wished I was more like the "life of the party" type of person. However, my *highly advanced* sense of humor literally ***forces*** others to enjoy my company. I have discovered from looking back over my life that people have always valued my input in important matters. When some people talk, you don't know how much of what they're saying to believe. They are constantly exaggerating. Rather than focus on the fact that I'm not the one who's the center of attention at the parties, I've noticed that when I do speak up in various situations, people seem to listen to me more than they listen to others. I believe this is due in part to my quiet personality.

Overall, I think because I am more quiet-natured, when I do give input, it seems to be taken more credible than others.

Strength: People take me serious. I don't talk the problem, or gossip, or I don't need to talk just to fill time.

Weakness: I can be boring to be around.

2

A man of knowledge uses words with restraint, and a man of understanding is even-tempered.

Even a fool is thought wise if he keeps silent, and discerning if he holds his tongue.

Proverbs 17:27-28 (NIV)

– Isaiah
Married
TV Director
28

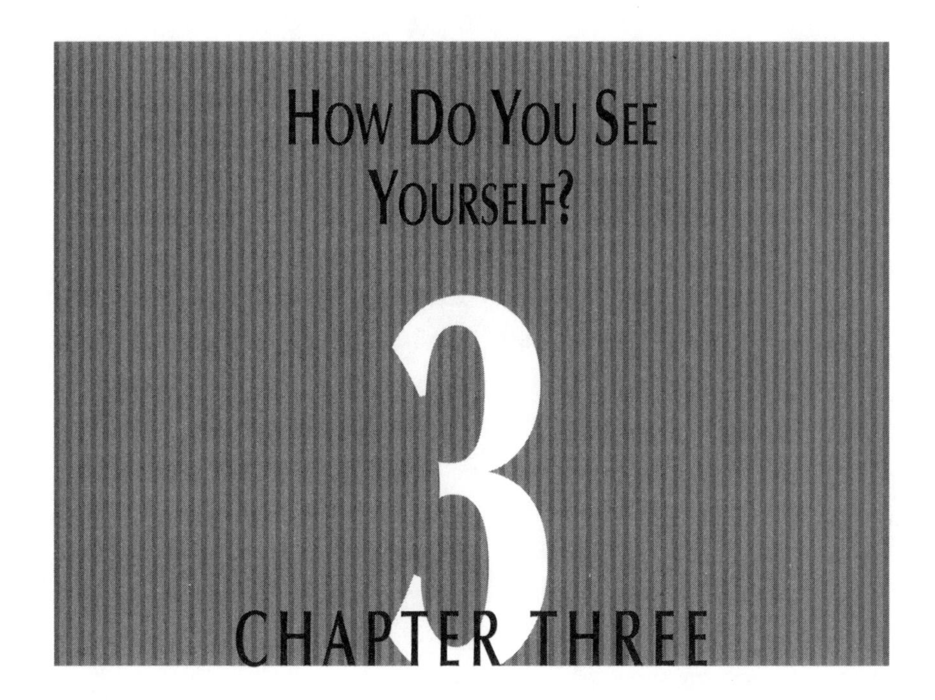

How Do You See Yourself?

Chapter Three

How you see yourself has everything to do with your destiny. I hope after reading that last chapter you are now convinced that God loves you. If not, read it again and again and again until you are convinced. In the eyes of God, your success is not dependent upon your circumstances. In the eyes of God, your success is dependent upon how you see yourself. If you think you're a failure, then you will fail. If you think you can win through the power of God that dwells within you, then you will win. It's up to you. It's your choice. You can either believe all the lies of the devil or you can believe what God says.

For as he thinketh in his heart, so is he . . .

Proverbs 23:7

Obviously, Satan wants to be the one to paint an image on the inside of you of the way you see yourself. For the most part, he's done a good job. I have to give him credit for that. But if you want to live in victory, then you must begin to discover God's image.

I didn't like myself

Some people don't like themselves. They don't like themselves for various reasons. I didn't like myself growing up, as I mentioned earlier, because I hated being little. Oh, I hated it. I figured my mom and dad had something to do with it so I was upset with them. Then they said something about God being the One Who made me and so I was really mad at Him. *Was He having a bad day? What was He thinking?*

It was not until I became an adult and surrendered my life to the Lord that I really started liking myself. When Carolyn and I got married, I had such a chip on my shoulder. I thought that if anybody looked at me then they must be thinking, "Look how little he is." I was very insecure.

Carolyn and I had only been married a week, and she called me in one day and said, "Jerry we have got too much trash in the house. Our garbage cans are filled. Let's take them outside." She said, "You grab one trash can and I will grab the other."

I said, "What's the matter? You don't think I can carry them both? I'm big enough to carry them both."

I related everything that was said to me as a remark about how little I was, and little meant weak, in my mind. I thought that people saw me as weak and not a man. I was always having to prove that I was as big as everybody else.

That is a terrible way to live when you go through life not liking yourself much less loving yourself. You have to fall in love with you. You have qualities that no one else has. You are unique. No one else can be exactly like you. Every person has something unique about them.

. . . Thou shalt love thy neighbor as thyself.

Matthew 19:19

How can you love your neighbor if you don't even love yourself? When you love yourself, then what you are saying is, *I accept me as who I am. God made me. I am not a mistake.* You don't put yourself down and condemn yourself when you love yourself. When you love yourself, you are saying, *I am worth something.* You are also saying, *I have something to offer.*

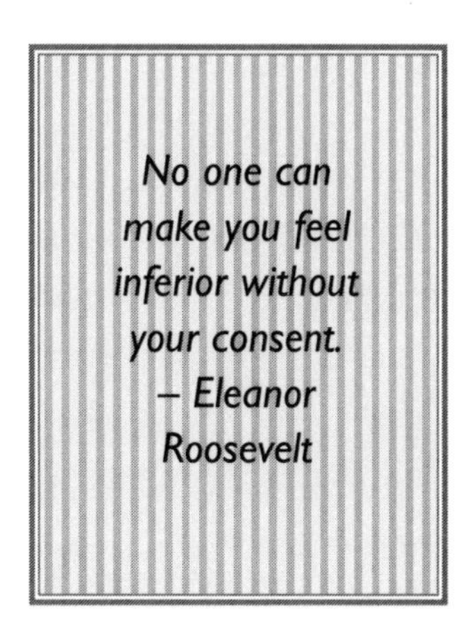

Healing for the hurts

By thinking and talking positive about yourself, you can bring healing to all the hurts and the wounds that you may have experienced over the years. Being called "little" wounded my spirit as a child. Like the first time I went out for Little League baseball and the coach told me "I am sorry son. You are too little." I went home crying. I sat in my bedroom and cried like a baby. I wanted to play baseball. I knew I could play as well as anybody out there but that coach did not even give me a chance. He just looked at my size and sent me home.

I was sitting on the floor crying, and then suddenly decided, *I will never cry again because crying means you're weak, and weak means you are little, weak people cry.* I sat there on the floor in my bedroom as a seven-year-old boy and I swore I would never cry again. I would spend the rest of my life, if I had to, proving I was as big as anybody else. My dad came home and said, "Son, how did it go in baseball today? Did you make the team?"

I said, "No, dad, they told me I was too little." He said, "Who told you that?" I said, "The coach. He didn't select me because he said I am too little. My dad sat down on the floor with me and said, "Well son, when I was your age I was little, too. They said the same thing about me too."

I know dad was trying to help, but it didn't help because I couldn't picture my dad as ever being little. I thought he was born an adult. My dad had big, broad shoulders, and big arms. If he was little when he was young, then something happened to him along the way because he got big. I didn't want to go back to school. I knew what I was going to get the next day. The boys that made the team were going to make fun of me because I was too little.

That next day, another coach came to our school and said, "We had so many boys try out for that team yesterday that we have decided to start another team." I said, "I am going out for that team and I am going to prove to them that I can play baseball as well as anyone out there." And they chose me. I was the starting pitcher and at the end of the season we played that other team for the championship with me as the pitcher and we won the game!

Shortly after we had won the game, that coach who told me I was too little came to my house and told my Dad, "I was wrong about your son. Will you ask him if he would like to try out for our team next year?" I heard the conversation, so I walked in the room with them. My dad said, "Son this man wants you to try out for his team." I said, "Dad, tell him I am too little," and I walked off. I never played for that coach and we ended up beating them every year.

It is terrible when you have to live your life under the words that somebody has spoken over you. They distort your image of yourself, but thank

God Jesus can heal you of hurtful words. God is a master at making champions out of nobodies. So start liking yourself. You have qualities. You have gifts. You have talents that God wants to use. Stay focused on what God says about you. If you will do that, then you will discover that He has a wonderful life for you.

You have to remember that when God sees you, He's looking through the Blood of Jesus. If there is anybody who believes in what happened at Calvary, it's God.

Once you discover God's image and God's opinion, then it's important that you accept it. Begin saying what He says about you. Stop calling yourself unworthy.

"Yea, but you don't know my past."

I don't have to know your past. What I need to know is that God thinks you are worthy. Once you accept God's opinion, then you'll be on your way to personal freedom.

We've all made mistakes. Big ones. Huge ones. Ones we wish so badly we could erase. In a perfect world, no one would ever make a mistake. But obviously, we don't live in a perfect world and you've probably already made more mistakes than you care to remember. I know I have.

On the other hand, the reason you are still not reaching your full potential is because you ***do*** remember all of your mistakes and you've never learned how to let go of them.

To enjoy the kind of success that God wants you to have, you must let go of yesterdays mistakes TODAY so that they won't have any affect on your tomorrow. To refuse to let go of yesterday's mistakes is to rob yourself of a better tomorrow. Satan is always looking for an advantage over you and holding onto your mistakes gives him one. And believe me, he will constantly remind you of it . . . if you let him.

It could be the very thing that is holding you back and you don't even realize it.

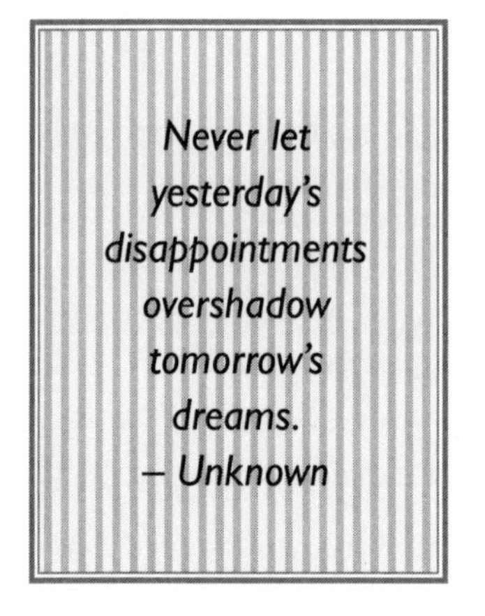

We've all made mistakes in our lives and we should take full responsibility for them, but hanging on to them will not make our lives better. At some point, ***you have to forgive yourself*** whether anyone else does or not.

What do you suppose would have become of a man named Peter if he had not forgiven himself for denying that he was one of the disciples of Jesus?

But Peter said unto him (Jesus)*, Although all shall be offended, yet will not I. And Jesus saith unto him, Verily I say unto thee, That this day, even in this night, before the cock crow twice, thou shalt deny me thrice. But he* (Peter) *spake the more vehemently, If I should die with thee, I will not deny thee in any wise. Likewise also said they all.*

Mark 14:29-31

Peter's denial of Jesus was foretold to him by Jesus Himself; however, Peter argued that this would never happen. But after Jesus was arrested "under pressure," Peter caved in.

And as Peter was beneath in the palace, there cometh one of the maids of the high priest. And when she saw Peter warming himself, she looked upon him, and said, And thou also wast with Jesus of Nazareth. But he denied, saying, I know not, neither understand I what thou sayest. And he went out into the porch; and the cock crew. And a maid saw him again, and began to say to them that stood by, This is one of them.

And he denied it again. And a little after, they that stood by said again to Peter, Surely thou art one of them: for thou art a Galilaean, and thy speech agreeth thereto. But he began to curse and to swear, saying, I know not this man of whom ye speak. And the second time the cock crew. And Peter called to mind the word that Jesus said unto him . . . And when he thought thereon, he wept.

Mark 14: 66-72

Obviously, he knew that he had made a horrible mistake. Can you imagine how difficult it must have been for Peter to forgive himself? He told Jesus he wouldn't deny Him, and he meant it . . . but under pressure, he gave in. I'm sure we've all "caved in" under pressure, and regretted it later. We meant well. We wanted to do the right thing, but we didn't. We've all been there.

Peter could have just as easily done what Judas did, commit suicide. Why? Because of the guilt and shame. The Bible tells us that Peter took this so hard, particularly after Jesus was crucified; that he left the other disciples and went back to fishing. He went back to his old lifestyle because he felt so "unworthy" to be called a "disciple."

But after Jesus was raised from the dead, the angel at the tomb said these words to Mary and the others there with her:

Free to be yourself

But go your way, tell his (Jesus) disciples <u>and Peter</u> that he goeth before you into Galilee: there shall ye see him, as he said unto you.

Mark 16:7

He actually called Peter BY NAME! It's obvious that Jesus had forgiven Peter, but could he forgive himself? Well, if you continue to read the Bible, you'll find that apparently, he did. And not only that, but he went on to become one of the "chief apostles" and was used mightily to spread the Gospel to the known world in those days.

If someone like Peter could let go of his past mistakes, then so can you. God can and wants to use you regardless of your past. He's already forgiven you if you've repented, but you have to forgive yourself. If you don't, then you'll never become all that God wants you to be.

You'll always be down on yourself and feeling like you're worthless. You'll constantly tell yourself that you can't be trusted with anything important because you'll probably "mess things up." Or you'll become so mentally paralyzed that you won't allow yourself to even think about taking a risk or stepping out in faith because you're afraid that you'll "blow it" again.

Obviously, your self-esteem is almost nonexistent. Now tell me, do you truly think that you'll ever enjoy any high degree of success when your life is in this condition? No, you won't! You have put yourself in a box. You've already determined your future. You've limited yourself to just existing – not living.

The abundant life that Jesus says is yours will never materialize if you refuse to let go of your mistakes. Let them go **<u>now</u>** and learn from them. Be wiser in the future; don't make the same mistakes twice. You have more information now than perhaps you had when you made the mistake.

Wisdom is the ability to use knowledge.

Apply the knowledge that you gained from this experience and get on with your life. Don't let what happened in the past hold you back any longer. It can absolutely paralyze your life.

Now, that doesn't mean that you can just keep on making the same mistakes. No, as I have previously stated; learn from them and then do your best not to make that same mistake again.

Look at your mistakes as new information about what works and what doesn't work. Learn from it and move on. The main thing is this: DON'T LET THEM HOLD YOU BACK.

The Apostle Paul (Saul as he was called then) made a major mistake – he consented to having Christians stoned to death or to be put in prison. He really thought that he was doing God a favor; however, it turned out to be a mistake.

But did he spend the rest of his life fretting over his mistake? No! He received forgiveness and he moved on with his life. And look what he accomplished!

Receive us; we have wronged no man, we have corrupted no man, we have defrauded no man.

II Corinthians 7:2

This reveals that he truly believed that God had forgiven him and that he truly, completely had forgiven himself. And aren't we glad that he did? Where would we be today without the teachings of this great man of God? What great and wonderful things are on the inside of you waiting to come out but your past is restricting you from being free? Even some of the greatest people you've ever heard about made mistakes. They got over theirs, now it's time for you to get over yours.

Remember ye not the former things, neither consider the things of old. Behold, I will do a new thing . . .

Isaiah 43:18-19

Behold, I am doing a new thing . . .

Isaiah 43:19 (Amplified)

In order for you to enjoy a bright future, it is absolutely necessary that you forget the past! No matter what Satan tries to tell you, according to the Word, you are a new creation in Christ Jesus and your past is forgiven. Satan can literally destroy your life by controlling your mind with thoughts about your past.

As you renew your mind, your old way of thinking will change. Your old habits and behavior patterns will be conformed to the will of God. Don't let Satan tell you that you're the same person you used to be. The past is the past. It's over. You are not that same person anymore. Today is a new day in your life.

. . . the accuser of our brethren . . .

Revelation 12:10

Satan likes to accuse you and bring guilt into your life to keep you down. He works overtime to try to keep you discouraged. He will constantly remind you of every wrong thing you've ever done. He hopes to keep you so low and so down on yourself that you will never be what God's called you to be.

Control your thoughts about yourself

Winners control their thoughts about themselves instead of allowing their thoughts to control them. Winners focus on what the Word says instead of what others say. Winners are not afraid to boldly declare who they are and what they are according to the Word of God even if some people don't agree with them. Your attitude about yourself can either make you or break you.

Let this mind be in you, which was also in Christ Jesus.

Philippians 2:5

Think of yourselves the way Christ Jesus thought of himself.

Philippians 2:5 (The Message Translation)

Many Christians do not have a revelation of who they are in Christ. If you never learn to see yourself the way God sees you, then Satan will torment your mind with insecurities and low self-esteem which will ultimately affect every area of your life.

When you believe what the Word says and make it final authority, then you'll begin to walk in a greater level of freedom than you've ever known in your life. When you learn who you are in Christ (like we discussed in chapter 2), then winning becomes your way of life. Losing becomes a thing of the past.

Therefore we are buried with him by baptism into death: that like as Christ was raised up from the dead by the glory of the Father, even so we also should walk in newness of life.

Romans 6:4

In other words, from that moment, you don't see yourself the way you used to see yourself. You don't see yourself the way other people see you. You begin to see yourself in Christ, and in Christ, you are a winner!

The first thing that you need to settle is this: God does not create failures. Let me repeat that: God does not create failures. It's not His nature to fail; and it's not His will for you to fail. When God made you, He saw a winner, not a loser.

If you can truly see yourself the way God sees you, then every limitation will be removed from your life. We saw in the last chapter that God has an opinion of you. His opinion of you is most likely different than the opinion you have had of yourself. Will you keep letting the devil defeat you through his lies about you, or are you going to accept God's opinion?

Mirror, mirror

But we all, with open face beholding as in a glass the glory of the Lord, are changed into the same image from glory to glory, even as by the Spirit of the Lord.

II Corinthians 3:18

Paul is telling us that God's Word is like a mirror. According to this verse, as we look in this mirror, we see the glory of the Lord. In other words, we see the image of Christ in this mirror. If we continue to look in this mirror, then we will be changed into that same image.

I'm sure that you looked in the mirror this morning and you saw an image. The image you saw was of yourself. That image may not have been what you wanted others to see, so you changed your image. In other words, you did what you felt was needed to be done in order to transform that image in the mirror into the one you wanted to see.

Transforming your image

The more you look into the Word, the more the image changes. Suddenly, you will not see yourself the way you used to see yourself. You will no longer see yourself the way others see you. You're going to see yourself the way God sees you.

Another word for ***changed*** is the word *transformed.* ***Transformed*** means *to change the shape and to change the appearance of.* Many times, if you go to a gym, they will have pictures of body-builders who, obviously, have spent a lot of time working out. Why do they put up pictures like that? To give you a vision of what can happen to you if you do what they did.

That's what God's Word is all about. God's Word is designed to paint a picture on the inside of you of the way God sees you. The image that God has of you will cause you to be changed.

The word ***transformed*** also means *metamorphosed.* It's like a caterpillar becoming a butterfly. Our self-image will go from feeling unworthy, shameful, and inferior to realizing we are a unique, special, and a one-of-a-kind child of God!

Transforming your thinking

. . . be ye transformed by the renewing of your mind . . .

Romans 12:2

How do you become transformed? By renewing your mind. You can't keep looking in the Word and see yourself failing – not when the Word says that you are more than a conqueror (Romans 8:37).

You will begin to see the image of a winner. It will cause you to get rid of all your negative thinking about yourself. It will destroy the sense of failure that perhaps you have carried around with you all of your life. It will remove all the guilt of your past.

Most of the people in the Bible were not qualified when God called them. They didn't have the right credentials. But God takes the foolish and confounds the wise. God takes what the world discards and turns them into champions. Praise God!!

Don't let Satan dictate your destiny. Don't allow him *to control* your self-image with thoughts of your past. Quit looking at the past. Everything you want or need is ahead of you. See yourself the way God sees you and you'll discover that you have unlimited potential.

If God can use me, he can use anybody. I look at men like Oral Roberts who was born as a stutterer. He could not speak well. He hated going to school because other kids made fun of him because he could hardly say his own name; and yet, God saw a diamond in the rough.

There is hope for each and every one of us. God can use anybody and He can use you. And He wants to use you. Moses said, "Who am I that I should bring forth the children of Israel out of Egypt?" That is quite a task. When you look at the task, when you look at how impossible that situation seemed, then you understand why Moses would say, "Who am I?" In the natural it was impossible, but God had chosen him to bring His people out of bondage. Moses felt inadequate, but God saw potential. Moses kept saying, "You don't understand." Have you ever said that to God?

How Do You See Yourself?

I have said many times that the greatest revelation you will ever get is "God is smarter than you." Yet we keep trying to tell God that He doesn't understand. God understands everything.

People with low self-esteem always see themselves incorrectly. When you have low self-esteem, you are never going to see yourself the way God sees you. At the Texas State Fair, they have what they call a fun house. When our daughters were young, we'd always visit the fun house. It has one of those distorted mirrors in it. You look in this mirror and it makes you look real long and skinny or real short and dumpy. You just look like you are as wide as the mirror. Well, that mirror was distorted. When you look in that mirror, you are not going to get a correct image. It is a distorted image. Well that is the way a lot of people see themselves.

You need to quit looking at yourself through that distorted mirror and go to the Word of God and allow that mirror to project an image of the way God sees you. If God thinks you are adequate, then you are adequate.

Like Moses, it will finally dawn on you that it is really not who you are but who God is. It is the greater One in us that makes the difference in our lives. It is not so much what I can do and who I am but it is who He is and what He can do. The Apostle Paul said, *I can do all things through Christ which strengtheneth me* (Philippians 4:13). Moses asked, "Who am I going to say sent me? God said, "Just tell them the I AM backs you" (Author's paraphrase).

In other words, we should believe that we can accomplish anything God says that we can when we know that He is backing us. Let me ask you a question. If you had been born into the John D. Rockefeller family, would it make a difference in your attitude today? Even little baby Rockefellers have a different attitude. They know they get the best cribs. They get the best milk. They get the best pacifiers. Well, I wasn't born a Rockefeller, but I was born of God. Even though the Rockefellers are quite wealthy people, they will never see the day that they will come close to God's capital reserve. We are born of Him.

Knowing this should have a profound affect on your attitude. It should cause you to hold your head up high, with a smile on your face because you know that God is backing you.

Don't say that!

As I have previously stated, you need to begin to see yourself the way God sees you. God does not consider you stupid, so quit calling yourself stupid. God does not consider you ugly, so don't call yourself ugly. Get rid of all those negative words that you have used on yourself. The Bible says you have the mind of Christ, so you couldn't be stupid. The Bible says you were intricately made, so you couldn't be ugly. If you are going to talk about yourself, then do so in terms of improvement but not cutting yourself down.

There is always room for improving ourselves but we don't have to be down on ourselves all the time. It is okay to say, "I need to stop procrastinating," but stop saying, "I am so lazy. I never get anything done on time." That kind of negative talk breeds other negative talk and the next thing you know everything you say about yourself will be negative.

Say things to motivate yourself to improve but not things that will pull yourself down all the time. It just grieves my spirit when I hear people do this. I have heard people do it with their children. "That kid is so stupid. I asked him to get bread and he gets milk." That child probably hears things like that all the time.

Unless that child discovers the Word of God, it is not likely that he will ever have any self-esteem. He will always see himself as stupid and ignorant and good for nothing. Why? Because that is what he has been told all his life, but thank God for the Bible. Thank God for the Word of God. You will never go to God and hear Him say, "Hey stupid. What can I do for you today?" He will never call you stupid. He will never call you ugly. He will never call you inadequate. He will never tell you that something is impossible. He will always say, "Come on. We can do this. I am with you. I am backing you. We can get the job done."

So it is important if you are going to be successful that you begin to develop a positive self-image. Confine your words about yourself to constructive criticism and not destructive criticism. Don't be down on yourself all the time. Recognize your weaknesses and endeavor to make yourself better, but don't continually use words that keep bringing you down. God doesn't condemn you so stop condemning yourself.

There is therefore no condemnation to them which are in Christ Jesus.

Romans 8:1

As far as God is concerned, the only one who can hold you back is you. Not even Satan can hold you back if you won't allow him. The only person who can keep you from enjoying a fulfilled and satisfied life is you. You are free to be the person God wants you to be.

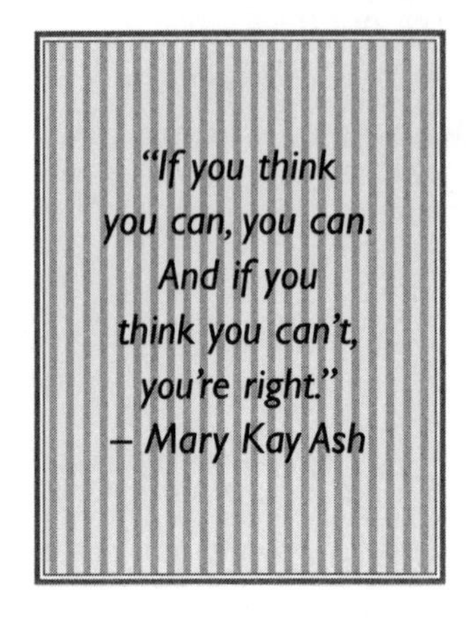

Satan is the one who is constantly trying to plant negative thoughts about yourself in your mind. You don't have to entertain them. The Bible says that you can cast them down. Commit yourself to be constantly on guard about negative thoughts. If you give Satan an inch, he will take a mile. If you sit around and allow him to put negative thoughts in your head for one minute, he will want an hour. If you give him an hour, he will want all day. The only way to stop him is to cast those thoughts down.

Wherefore gird up the loins of your mind . . .

I Peter 1:13

So brace up your minds; be sober (circumspect, morally alert) . . .

I Peter 1:13 (Amplified)

You have got to be alert. You have got to be attentive. You have to be on guard at all times. Have you ever been sitting in a church service and all of a sudden, the dumbest, most negative thought just flashes across your mind and you think, *Where did that come from?* You could be sitting in the most inspiring service you have ever been to in your life and Satan will try to get a negative thought in. He will try to tell you before you leave the building *that is all well and good but after all, that will never work for you.* You have to cast those thoughts down.

You don't have to allow those thoughts to stay in your mind. You have the authority to be selective about what you think. When Peter says, *Gird up the loins of your mind or brace your mind and be alert,* he is saying **take**

this seriously. This is vital to your success. You cannot allow Satan to use your mind as his playground because he will talk you into losing, giving up, being defeated, and living way below your privileges as a child of God. For every negative thought that comes into your mind, you must learn to speak positive words as a rebuttal. The moment the negative thought comes in, you must begin to speak the Word of God **out loud.**

You cannot say out loud what God says and keep thinking what the devil says at the same time. This is how you resist the devil as written in James 4:7 – . . . *Resist the devil, and he will flee from you.* The Amplified Bible says, . . . *stand firm against him . . .*

Let him know that he has no right to control your thoughts. He has no right to make you think his thoughts. Let him know that Jesus is your Lord and His thoughts are the thoughts that you choose to think.

Smith Wigglesworth was standing on a corner one time waiting to get on a tram or a train in England. A lady who had a little dog was waiting also. The little dog had followed her but when the tram arrived, the woman said, "Go on home, sweetheart. Go on home. You can't go with me today." The little dog just stood there and looked at her and wagged his tail. He didn't pay any attention to her. She said, "Now get on home, sweetheart. You have to go back home, you cannot go with me today." Mr. Wigglesworth was just standing there watching all of this. She did that about three or four times and the dog still paid no attention to her.

Finally, she stomped her foot and with a loud voice said, "Get!" And that dog took off! Smith Wigglesworth just shouted, "That's the way you have to do the devil!"

He is not a gentleman and he won't leave on his own. You can't say, "Please Mr. Devil, don't put another negative thought in my mind." He won't respond to that. He only responds to authority. You have to be firm with him. You have to be bold about it and tell him that your mind is not going to be his playground today. Tell him that you choose to think the thoughts of God.

3

"I was a big dreamer but never put the dreams into action!"

Defeating the fear of failing

Meet Cheryl . . .

As the pressures of high school drew near – you wonder as a teenager, "What am I going to do with the rest of my life?" The theme that resonated throughout high school was that in everything you do – we all have the power of choice. The saying is true about what a person does and decides in the present day will affect and guide the relations for the future. I guess you could say that I was a big dreamer growing up, however I never thought to put those dreams or thoughts into action. Most people leave the dreams at the foot of the bed and follow reality out the door.

As far as I can remember, music has been an integral part of my life. I listened to all kinds of music growing up, yet there is something saintly powerful about Christian music. The expression of words and encouragements that the artists take on musically help captivate and spread the joy that Christian music can bring into many lives. The very essence of such music has powerful effects in just about every dimension of our lives, whether we know it or not.

Thoughts clouded my head with negative imagery of failure of what others would think, and how they would react based on the dreams and desires I set out to accomplish.

On that day of commencement, I can remember thinking, *What will I most likely be doing ten years from now?* I had so many dreams and avenues that I wanted to try and **I was scared of failing** at any or all of them for that matter. Sometimes many people find themselves in a holding pattern of what to do, and where to go, and how to get there.

I often think back to the time when three young men penetrated onto the Christian music scene around the time I was trying to figure out which path to take. These men had a fresh new and innovative sound and style that was exploding in the Christian music arena. Their boldness and heart for God took on a newfound precedent among young people everywhere and I was no exception. The youthful age of my generation had arose to this newness that laid dormant for so long. Deep down, I felt many passions rising up within me and screaming to make known what my soul was feeling for so long. The gallant hearts of these young men had pinched a nerve within me, itching to get to the surface of something greater in my life. My goal that stemmed from these inner desires that were brought to the surface somehow put a tinge of fear inside me.

As of today, I am still involved in what I set out to do more than ten years ago. As the years have passed, my desires are set in full swing about to embark on the next level of accomplishments. For the young and old, **never give up on one's own dreams,** and as Christians encourage each other to strive for the best, and to be the best in His excellence. Remember yesterday is history (learn and grow from the decision whether good or bad), and tomorrow is a mystery, and today is a gift.

– Cheryl
Single
Royalty Administrator
33

How Do Others See You?

by Terri Savelle Foy

4 CHAPTER FOUR

Your first response might be, "I don't want to know," or "I don't really care." But the fact is that people do see you a certain way and it may or may not be different from the way you see yourself. It can be very helpful and motivating to discover the way you are perceived by others. It builds your confidence when you find out which of your traits seem to *stand out* the most and it will encourage you even more in your quest to be free to be yourself.

On the other hand, people may have a wrong perception of you based on what they've been told or their perception of you is based on who you were "before Christ." That's not who you are anymore. I'm referring to the people around you right now who recognize your strengths and character traits on a consistent basis.

Not too long ago, my family was flying back from one of our "Up Close and Personal" meetings we conduct as a family. My "deep, psychological sister" said, "Let's play a game. Let's all list three strengths that we see in each other."

After rolling my eyes and hearing the sighs of my parents, we all agreed to play *her little game.* In doing so, it actually turned into a very emotional and intimate time with my family that was precious to each of us.

What I realized as I listened to my family describe my strengths, was that the first thing my Dad mentioned about me was not something I've ever noticed about myself. It's not even something I intentionally "tried to be" or "tried to do." I guess it's just me being myself . . . and others noticed it as a strength. Now that I'm aware of it, I feel more confident in that area . . . to be me.

The people around you see things in you that you may not even see in yourself. Some people see how you conduct yourself in private and in public settings. They see how you wake up and how you are before you go to bed. And it's not all bad! Our first reaction is to criticize the negative things about ourselves rather than say, "Hey, maybe I do have some strengths that I've never really noticed."

What is that familiar saying about compliments? It takes seven compliments to override one negative remark. I think so many times you hear what others don't like about you or things that irritate them about you, and the only time you hear all these wonderful "strengths" about a person is at their funeral! And they aren't even "there" to appreciate it!

That day in the airplane, I even told my family how encouraging it was to know that they see me that way, and I was alive to hear it!

Not only will it encourage you to discover how others see you, but it will inspire you to like yourself and be free to enjoy those things about you. It's just a part of who you are, your overall make up, and it actually fits in with God's assignment on your life!

I encourage you to sit down with your closest friends and family, and do like my sister did, make a game out of it. Before everyone starts acting like this is their moment to "tear into you" – remind them that you are focusing on three "strengths" you see in each other. Be sure to let them talk. Don't remind them of how good you are at something. Just sit there quietly and listen. These are the first three strengths that come to their mind when they think of you.

Get out your pen and paper and write it all down. Give the list to each person so they can keep it and be reminded that they do have *at least* three wonderful traits. Look at it from time to time. It will keep you encouraged and will help your self-esteem rise.

The first word that comes to mind

Being a senior vice president at Jerry Savelle Ministries, along with my sister, I directly oversee all of the Media and Communication Departments. One day in our Media Team meetings, we were discussing the image of our ministry. Our marketing director wanted to get a clear representation of our image on paper.

So, she began asking, "What is the first word that comes to your mind when you think of Jerry Savelle?" All around the room, people began to just blurt it out. It was so interesting to hear how many people had the same first word describing him: ***down-to-earth!***

We were amazed that so many of us thought the exact same thing. We then asked for more words describing him and we put them all together on one board that we actually keep hanging in our media room. It keeps us focused on our image and helps us design every marketing piece around that image.

Why is that helpful? Again, seeing how you are perceived by others may be different than the way you perceive yourself. Their perceptions can be very encouraging and enlightening. Once you realize how you are perceived, and you recognize it as simply who you are to the outside world, it gives you a certain freedom to be confident.

After meeting with my Dad and presenting the "image board" to him to see what he thought, he wasn't shocked or surprised. At the same time, I don't think he had ever "consciously" thought of himself in those words. I'm positive that he never saw how others perceive him ***written down.***

When you recognize how others see you and you hear the words describing you, it releases you from the struggle of trying to be something you're not and enables you to embrace who you are. Sure, there are things we will always be striving to improve about ourselves, but I'm referring to the natural, everyday person that you are and the personality that you have.

I've even seen my dad appear more comfortable in recognizing that he represents the ***average person***. His style of preaching is down to earth and easy to understand. When you know that you are perceived a certain way, then there is no need to try to be different. In fact, that is why people like you. That could be the very thing that draws others to you.

Perception equals reality

It's been said that "perception equals reality." So, ask around. Ask the people who know you, have spent time with you, and are familiar with exactly who you are.

As they begin to share their "first few words" describing you, stay quiet and just write it all down. Once you see all of these descriptions written down, enjoy this newfound knowledge. Don't allow yourself to start criticizing words that you don't think should be there. Look at the positive side of those words and look at it as something God put in you . . . for a reason.

I remember one time when a person described me as "quiet-natured, funny, and timid . . ." I thought, *"Timid? I don't like that word."* Then, they began to explain that what they were trying to say is that I am soft-spoken and my voice can make me appear shy . . . until you get to know me.

Once they explained what they meant by that word, I was okay with it. So, you might need to ask them to "expound" as to why they use a certain word. It could just be that they don't really know the *right* word they're trying to say. Please . . . don't allow yourself to get offended. This book is designed to "set you free" not put you in bondage!

Seeing how others perceive you and hearing the first few words used to describe you should be motivating. I think we've all questioned at times in our mind, "I wonder what they think about me?" Well, I've discovered that you can't stop people from thinking things about you no matter how hard you try, so why not ask? This will clear up the wondering.

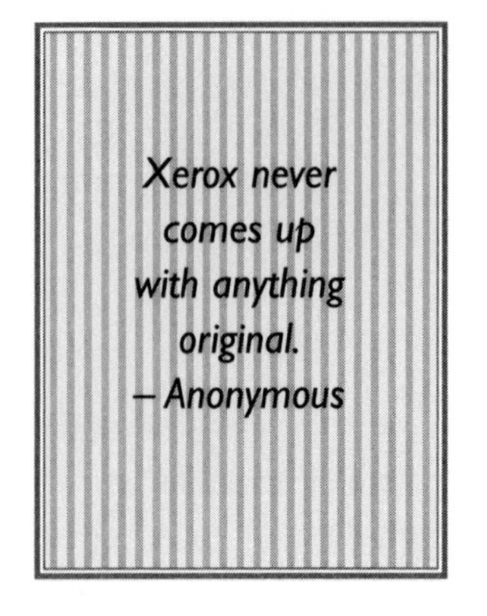

So, set a meeting with your closest friends and listen. Again, if you hear a word that sounds bad to your ears, ask them to explain. If you're being described as "bold," don't look at that in the negative sense. Jesus wants us to be "bold as lions." Be cautious of immediately focusing on the negative outlook of the words used. Look at them as positive feedback on the God-given nature and personality that you have.

At the same time, keeping in mind that your self-image isn't based on what others think about you, it is based on what God thinks and He thinks you're wonderful, unique, chosen, and one-of-a-kind.

4

"I had a fear of public speaking!"

Pastor overcomes nerves and gains confidence

Meet Pastor Bob . . .

When God called me to preach, the biggest reservation that I had was a fear of public speaking. When I had to speak before a crowd, I would get very nervous and uncomfortable. I told God that I couldn't preach because **it was such a crisis for me every time I had to speak to a group.** Nevertheless, while I was in college I preached on weekends at small churches and every time I would preach, I would have to spend much time in prayer beforehand to have the confidence that **I needed** to speak before a group.

This fear continued for the first 20 times that I preached and then one day it left. I did what Joyce Meyers says in her book, "Do It Afraid". Unfortunately, I didn't have Joyce's book to read back then. I did it afraid until the fear left. Now I preach over 100 times a year to a congregation of over 300 people. And when our church has had well-known speakers, I've had to speak before over 1,000 people. I have no fear because **I conquered that fear of public speaking** by refusing to give in to it. Now I regularly make a fool of myself before large groups of people and think nothing of it. Fear is a spirit sent to stop us from doing the will of God and we defeat it by refusing to listen to it and obey it. The number one command in the Bible is "fear not." What fear is stopping you from fulfilling your destiny? Don't give in to it and let it stop you. God didn't give us a spirit of fear, but a spirit of power, love, and a sound mind.

– Bob
Married with two children
Pastor
46

What Is Your Personality Type?

by Jerriann Savelle Bridges

5

CHAPTER FIVE

A few years ago, I had my family over for Thanksgiving dinner. In typical fashion for being the "deep" one in the family, I gave everyone a personality quiz. I have always been intrigued by different personality types. When I began studying that God has made each one of us with a special and unique personality, it really began to shed light on why we are the way we are.

By giving everyone this test and then discussing it, it began to make so much sense. I never understood how my sister and I were born in the same household, but saw (and reacted to) most things so differently. Through studying the personality profiles, I discovered that it is because we are not the same personalities. In fact, we are exact opposites! God didn't make us the same for a reason and now that we work together in ministry, we see the purpose behind it all. It takes both types of personalities to do what we do.

I tried so hard to be quiet and gentle, but I'm a Choleric personality.

Choleric's are leaders; they are the movers and the shakers. I am a leader and that's just the way God "wired" me. There is no right or wrong personality. God has created us exactly the way He wants us to be. Yes, we all have areas of growth and improvement (some of us more than others), but God gave us each the personality He wanted us to have.

My mother used to always say, in frustration of my stubbornness while I was growing up, "Jerri, if you would just direct that leadership ability in the right direction ..." and I finally did. We can't make ourselves something we aren't, we can only work on refining the weaknesses, which I believe is a lifetime process.

I've often said that I wish I had had this knowledge years ago, I would not have been so bound, and battled with insecurities, had I really known that God made me with THIS personality. It's so freeing to truly find that out!

I encourage you to take this "Personality Profile" quiz "Used with permission from the book *Personality Plus* by Florence Littauer. For more information on the Personality Types as taught by Florence Littauer or to order *Personality Plus* please call 1-800-433-6633 or visit www.thepersonalities.com." And I believe you will learn from the personality descriptions taken from *The Spirit-Controlled Temperament* by Tim LaHaye (Tyndale House Publishers, Inc. Used by Permission.) I believe it will help you in discovering why you are the way you are and help you accept yourself and your personality.

Your Personality Profile (Florence Littauer)

Directions – In each of the following rows of four words *across,* place an X in front of the one word that most often applies to you. Continue through all forty lines; be sure each number is marked. If you are not sure which word "most applies," ask a spouse or a friend, and think of what your answer would have been when *you were* a child.

STRENGTHS

1	___Adventurous	___Adaptable	___Animated	___Analytical
2	___Persistent	___Playful	___Persuasive	___Peaceful
3	___Submissive	___Self-sacrificing	___Sociable	___Strong-willed
4	___Considerate	___Controlled	___Competitive	___Convincing
5	___Refreshing	___Respectful	___Reserved	___Resourceful
6	___Satisfied	___Sensitive	___Self-reliant	___Spirited
7	___Planner	___Patient	___Positive	___Promoter
8	___Sure	___Spontaneous	___Scheduled	___Shy
9	___Orderly	___Obliging	___Outspoken	___Optimistic
10	___Friendly	___Faithful	___Funny	___Forceful
11	___Daring	___Delightful	___Diplomatic	___Detailed
12	___Cheerful	___Consistent	___Cultured	___Confident
13	___Idealistic	___Independent	___Inoffensive	___Inspiring
14	___Demonstrative	___Decisive	___Dry humor	___Deep
15	___Mediator	___Musical	___Mover	___Mixes easily
16	___Thoughtful	___Tenacious	___Talker	___Tolerant
17	___Listener	___Loyal	___Leader	___Lively
18	___Contented	___Chief	___Chartmaker	___Cute
19	___Perfectionist	___Pleasant	___Productive	___Popular
20	___Bouncy	___Bold	___Behaved	___Balanced

WEAKNESSES

21	___Blank	___Bashful	___Brassy	___Bossy
22	___Undisciplined	___Unsympathetic	___Unenthusiastic	___Unforgiving
23	___Reticent	___Resentful	___Resistant	___Repetitious
24	___Fussy	___Fearful	___Forgetful	___Frank
25	___Impatient	___Insecure	___Indecisive	___Interrupts
26	___Unpopular	___Uninvolved	___Unpredictable	___Unaffectionate
27	___Headstrong	___Haphazard	___Hard to please	___Hesitant
28	___Plain	___Pessimistic	___Proud	___Permissive
29	___Angered easily	___Aimless	___Argumentative	___Alienated
30	___Naive	___Negative attitude	___Nervy	___Nonchalant
31	___Worrier	___Withdrawn	___Workaholic	___Wants credit
32	___Too sensitive	___Tactless	___Timid	___Talkative
33	___Doubtful	___Disorganized	___Domineering	___Depressed
34	___Inconsistent	___Introvert	___Intolerant	___Indifferent
35	___Messy	___Moody	___Mumbles	___Manipulative
36	___Slow	___Stubborn	___Show-off	___Skeptical
37	___Loner	___Lord over others	___ Lazy	___Loud
38	___Sluggish	___Suspicious	___Short-tempered	___Scatterbrained
39	___Revengeful	___Restless	___Reluctant	___Rash
40	___Compromising	___Critical	___Crafty	___Changeable

Personality Scoring Sheet

Now transfer all your Xs to the corresponding words on the Personality Scoring Sheet and add up your totals. For example, if you checked Animated on the profile, check it on the scoring sheet. (Note: The words are in a different order on the profile and the scoring sheet.)

STRENGTHS

	Sparky Sanguine	Rocky Choleric	Maestro Melancholy	Flip Phlegmatic
1	__Animated	__Adventurous	__Analytical	__Adaptable
2	__Playful	__Persuasive	__Persistent	__Peaceful
3	__Sociable	__Strong-willed	__Self-sacrificing	__Submissive
4	__Convincing	__Competitive	__Considerate	__Controlled
5	__Refreshing	__Resourceful	__Respectful	__Reserved
6	__Spirited	__Self-reliant	__Sensitive	__Satisfied
7	__Promoter	__Positive	__Planner	__Patient
8	__Spontaneous	__Sure	__Scheduled	__Shy
9	__Optimistic	__Outspoken	__Orderly	__Obliging
10	__Funny	__Forceful	__Faithful	__Friendly
11	__Delightful	__Daring	__Detailed	__Diplomatic
12	__Cheerful	__Confident	__Cultured	__Consistent
13	__Inspiring	__Independent	__Idealistic	__Inoffensive
14	__Demonstrative	__Decisive	__Deep	__Dry humor
15	__Mixes easily	__Mover	__Musical	__Mediator
16	__Talker	__Tenacious	__Thoughtful	__Tolerant
17	__Lively	__Leader	__Loyal	__Listener
18	__Cute	__Chief	__Chartmaker	__Contented
19	__Popular	__Productive	__Perfectionist	__Pleasant
20	__Bouncy	__Bold	__Behaved	__Balanced

TOTALS – STRENGTHS

______	______	______	______

WEAKNESSES

	Sparky Sanguine	Rocky Choleric	Maestro Melancholy	Flip Phlegmatic
21	__Brassy	__Bossy	__Bashful	__Blank
22	__Undisciplined	__Unsympathetic	__Unforgiving	__Unenthusiastic
23	__Repetitious	__Resistant	__Resentful	__Reticent
24	__Forgetful	__Frank	__Fussy	__Fearful
25	__Interrupts	__Impatient	__Insecure	__Indecisive
26	__Unpredictable	__Unaffectionate	__Unpopular	__Uninvolved
27	__Haphazard	__Headstrong	__Hard to please	__Hesitant
28	__Permissive	__Proud	__Pessimistic	__Plain
29	__Angered easily	__Argumentative	__Alienated	__Aimless
30	__Naive	__Nervy	__Negative attitude	__Nonchalant
31	__Wants credit	__Workaholic	__Withdrawn	__Worrier
32	__Talkative	__Tactless	__Too sensitive	__Timid
33	__Disorganized	__Domineering	__Depressed	__Doubtful
34	__Inconsistent	__Intolerant	__Introvert	__Indifferent
35	__Messy	__Manipulative	__Moody	__Mumbles
36	__Show-off	__Stubborn	__Skeptical	__Slow
37	__Loud	__Lord over others	__ Loner	__Lazy
38	__Scatterbrained	__Short-tempered	__Suspicious	__Sluggish
39	__Restless	__Rash	__Revengeful	__Reluctant
40	__Changeable	__Crafty	__Critical	__Compromising

TOTALS – WEAKNESSES

_______	_______	_______	_______

COMBINED TOTALS

_______	_______	_______	_______

The Four Basic Temperaments (Tim LaHaye)

Sparky Sanguine

Sparky Sanguine is the warm, buoyant, lively, and fun-loving temperament. He is receptive by nature, and external impressions easily find their way to his heart, where they readily cause an outburst of response. Feelings rather than reflective thoughts predominate to form his decisions.

Sparky Sanguine has an unusual capacity to enjoy himself and usually passes on his hearty outgoing nature. When he comes into a room of people, he has a tendency to lift the spirits of everyone present by his exuberant flow of conversation. He is a thrilling storyteller because his warm, emotional nature almost makes him relive the experience in the very telling of it.

Sparky Sanguine never lacks for friends. In *Temperament and the Christian Faith,* Dr. Hallesby said, "His naive, spontaneous, genial nature opens doors and hearts to him." He can genuinely feel the joys and sorrows of the person he meets and has the capacity to make that person feel important, as though the new acquaintance were a very special friend, which he or she is – until Sparky meets the next person, who then receives the same attention.

Without any malice, Sparky might forget his resolutions, appointments, and obligations. He's on to the next exciting adventure, which makes him seem unstable.

Sparky does not like solitude but enjoys people and is at his best surrounded by friends, where he is the life of the party. He has an endless repertoire of interesting stories that he tells dramatically, making him a favorite with children as well as adults and usually gaining him admission at the best parties or social gatherings.

The Sanguine is never at a loss for words, though he often speaks without thinking. His open sincerity, however, has a disarming effect on many of his listeners, causing them to respond to his mood. His free-wheeling, seemingly exciting, extrovertish way of life makes him the envy of the more timid temperament types.

Habits of temperament

Temperament affects basic habits of living – the way we drive, keep the yard, and eat, for example. Driving habits of Sanguines? In a word, erratic. Sometimes they speed, then for no apparent reason they lose interest in driving fast and slow down. Riding in the backseat of a Sanguine's car can be downright dangerous. They are so people-oriented that they want to look you – the passenger – in the face while driving. Being super talkers, they spend very little time watching where they are going.

As for yard care, Sparky Sanguine gets up early Saturday morning to fix his yard. With great gusto he lines up all his tools (he has every gadget known to man because he totally lacks sales resistance) and prepares to cut, trim, shear, and prune. But within thirty minutes his wife can't hear a sound outside. Looking down the street, she sees him chatting with a neighbor. Before the day is over, he orders his son to "put my tools away" and decides to fix the yard next week. Sparky is clearly one of the world's great procrastinators.

Eating habits? Sanguines eat everything in sight – and usually look it. Incidentally, in restaurants they almost never look at the menu until the waitress arrives; they've been enjoying the conversation too much.

Balancing a checkbook? Sanguines can rarely find theirs and don't always remember to write amounts in the right place or balance the accounts. I have never met a Sanguine accountant.

A Biblical Sanguine

The Apostle Peter was a Sanguine. Every time he appeared in the Gospels, he was talking. In fact, I read through the Gospels one time to verify my suspicion and found that Simon Peter the Sanguine talked more than all the other disciples put together. As my minister friend Ken Poure says, "A Sanguine enters a room mouth first." And like most Sanguines, Ken Poure is loved by everyone.

Their noisy, blustering, friendly ways make Sanguines appear more confident than they really are, but their energy and lovable disposition get them by the rough spots of life.

People have a way of excusing their weaknesses by saying, "That's just the way they are."

As for the Apostle Peter: Everything he said in the Gospels was "wrong" except his great confession of Christ's deity (see Matt. 16:16). His sinful betrayal and easy repentance "with tears" is typically Sanguine. They always feel bad for wrong-doing – after they get caught. But that is not the end of the story! Peter became the strong, resolute leader of the early church. In the Acts of the Apostles, everything he said was right – because he was filled with the Holy Spirit.

Career bests

The world is enriched by these cheerful Sanguines with their natural charisma. They usually make excellent salespeople and more than other groups seem attracted to that profession. You have doubtless heard this cliche: "He could sell refrigerators to the Eskimos." That's Sparky. If you ever want to watch Mr. Sanguine in action, just visit your local used-car dealer. About two-thirds of his salesreps seem to be Sanguines.

In addition to being good at sales, Sanguines make excellent actors, entertainers, and preachers (particularly evangelists). They are outstanding masters of ceremonies, auctioneers, and sometimes leaders (if properly blended with another temperament). Because of our mass media today, they are increasingly in demand within the political arena, where natural charisma has proved advantageous.

In the area of helping people, Sanguines excel as hospital workers. Most sick people respond to Nurse Sanguine's "How are you today?" by saying, "Fine," while Nurse Melancholy asking the same question would probably receive the self-pitying lament, "Miserable." You may be on the verge of death, as white as the sheet you are lying on when Dr. Sanguine bubbles into your room; but before the doctor leaves, your spirits will be lifted. This doctor's obvious compassion in response to your tale of woe will almost make paying his exorbitant bill easy. (Sanguines are never moderate about anything.)

Sanguines should choose careers that allow them extensive exposure to people. I think their chief contribution to life lies in making other people happy. Certainly someone should be assigned that task in these uncertain times.

Now meet the second temperament type . . .

Rocky Choleric

Rocky Choleric is the hot, quick, active, practical, and strong-willed temperament. He is often self-sufficient and very independent. He tends to be decisive and opinionated, finding it easy to make decisions for himself as well as for others.

Rocky Choleric thrives on activity. In fact, to him, "life is activity." He does not need to be stimulated by his environment. No, he stimulates the environment with his endless ideas, plans, and ambitions. His is not an aimless activity, for he has a practical, keen mind, capable of making sound, instant decisions or planning worthwhile, long-range projects. He does not vacillate under pressure of what others think. He takes a definite stand on issues and can often be found crusading against social injustice or unhealthy situations.

He is not frightened by adversities; in fact, they tend to encourage him. He has dogged determination and often succeeds where others fail – not because his plans are better than others, but because he is still "pushing ahead" after others have become discouraged and quit. If there is any truth in the adage "Leaders are born, not made," then the Choleric is a born leader. He always lands on his feet.

Rocky Choleric's emotional nature is the least developed part of his temperament. He does not sympathize easily with others, nor does he naturally show or express compassion. He is often embarrassed or disgusted by the tears of others. He has little appreciation for the fine arts; his primary interest is in the utilitarian values of life. He is so optimistic, rarely anticipating failure, that he seldom fails – except at home. Love is not usually high on his priority list.

He is quick to recognize opportunities and equally as quick at diagnosing the best way to make use of them. He has a well-organized mind, though details usually bore him. He is not given to analysis but to quick, almost intuitive appraisal; that means he tends to look at the goal toward which he is working without seeing the potential pitfalls and obstacles in the path. Once he has started toward a goal, he may run roughshod over individuals that stand in his way. He tends to be domineering and bossy and does not hesitate to use people to accomplish his ends. He is often considered an opportunist.

The Choleric's attitude of self-sufficiency and willfulness makes him difficult to reach for Christ in adulthood. For this reason I urge Sunday school teachers, "Never let a fifth-grade Choleric out of your class until that child has found Christ as Lord and Savior." That is also good advice for parents. The more Choleric your children's temperaments, the more intense should be your prayers for their conversion between third and fifth grade, while they still retain sensitivity to spiritual things.

Habits of temperament

Let's look at the same habits we considered for the Sanguine. Behind the wheel, Cholerics are daring speed demons who dart in and out of traffic constantly. They always try to get more accomplished in a given period of time than is humanly possible and attempt to make up time by driving furiously between appointments. Strangely enough, they rarely get tickets – not because they don't deserve them, but because they are crafty enough to keep an eye on the rearview mirror to watch for the local "black and white."

Rocky Choleric hates yard work. When he does it at all, it is with a vengeance. He is not mechanical by nature and detests repairs or pruning because, quite frankly, he is not very good at it. When he does take on the yard, he works at a frenzied pace to get the job done, but neatness is not his hallmark. In fact, the family of a Choleric should never let him prune bushes, trees, or hedges, for he has only one idea in mind – "If you have to do it, you might as well do it once for the whole year!" One can usually spot the Choleric's yard while driving through the neighborhood. Just look for miniature hedges and dwarf trees.

Cholerics are stereotyped eaters – their menu seldom varies from one day to the next, and when their food arrives, they bolt it down in big chunks, often talking while chewing. Frequently they are the first ones finished.

Balancing a checkbook? Cholerics hate details, so they assign or hire someone else to take care of it or carry two accounts – using one for six months, then shifting to the other so they don't bounce any checks.

Career bests

Cholerics might consider careers that require leadership, motivation, and productivity, provided they do not require too much attention to details and analytical planning. Committee meetings and long-range planning bore the Choleric – a doer. Rarely will you find a predominant Choleric as a surgeon, dentist, philosopher, inventor, or watchmaker. Although not usually craftsmen (requiring a degree of perfection and efficiency usually beyond their capability), Cholerics often supervise craftsmen. They usually enjoy construction work, because it is so productive, and will frequently end up being foremen or project supervisors.

Rocky Choleric is a developer by nature. When he drives through the countryside, he cannot share his passenger's enjoyment of the "beautiful rolling hillsides," for he envisions road graders carving out streets and builders constructing homes, schools, and shopping centers.

Most of today's cities and suburbs were first envisioned by a Choleric. You can be sure, however, that he hired a Melancholy as the architect with the analytical and creative ability to draw the plans he outlined. He can't fully understand why a few lines on the back of an envelope aren't sufficient to gain the city planning department's approval. No one fights city hall harder than a Choleric, who bitterly laments, why all this business of detailed plans, anyway? "I've built enough projects to know that the best plans have to be modified during construction, so why not make up your mind as you go along on the little issues? I know what I want to accomplish!"

So wise Choleric hires a Melancholy assistant or goes into business partnership with a Melancholy. Together they make an unbeatable team. Of course, since everyone has both a primary and secondary temperament, occasionally you might meet a person with both traits.

Most entrepreneurs are Cholerics. They formulate the ideas and are venturesome enough to launch out in new directions. They don't limit themselves to their own ideas either but sometimes overhear a creative idea from someone not sufficiently adventurous to initiate a new business, however, they are likely to get bored soon after its success.

There are two reasons for this. First, as the business it creates more detail work. But since Cholerics are not by nature good delegators of responsibility (although with proper training they can learn) and like to see the fruits of their own productive and capable industry, they tend to evaluate negatively the efforts of others. Consequently, they end up trying to do everything themselves.

Second, when Cholerics discover that they are "just too busy," they look for someone to buy their businesses. So the average Choleric can be expected to start four to ten businesses or organizations in a lifetime.

Once Cholerics learn to delegate responsibility to and discover that they are able to accomplish more through other people, they can complete an amazing amount of work. Other people cannot believe that Cholerics can be involved in so many things and keep their sanity.

Well, here's how they do it. Since they are completely performance-conscious and have no perfectionist hang-ups, they reason, *I'd rather get a number of things, 70 to 80, finished than a few things, 100 percent, completed.*

Rocky Choleric is a natural motivator of other people. He oozes self-confidence, is extremely goal-conscious, and can inspire others to envision his goals. Consequently, associates may find themselves more productive by following the Choleric's lead. His primary weakness as a leader is that he is hard to please and tends to run roughshod over other people. If he only knew how others look to him for approval and encouragement, he would spend more time patting them on the back, which would generate even greater dedication from them. But the Choleric subconsciously thinks that approval and encouragement will lead to complacency; he assumes that an employee's productivity will fall off if he is too complimentary. So he resorts to criticism in the hope that this will inspire greater effort. (Unfortunately it doesn't.)

Cholerics have a built-in promotional ability and do well in sales, teaching (but always practical subjects), politics, with military service, sports, and many other endeavors.

Like the Sanguine, Rocky Choleric makes a good preacher, although he is much less emotional. I have noticed that many of the most successful churches in the country are led by Choleric preachers – dynamic Bible teachers with organizational and promotional abilities and strong leadership gifts. They're not afraid to launch into projects and, with proper motivation and the blessing of God, usually enjoy a successful ministry.

Western civilization has benefited much from its Rocky Cholerics. But it has suffered much from them also. The world's greatest generals, dictators, and gangsters have been predominantly Choleric. What made the difference? Their moral values and motivations. If there is such a thing as a success tendency, Cholerics have it. That doesn't mean they are smarter than other people, as is often assumed, but that their strong will and determination drive them to succeed where other, more gifted, people are prone to give up.

A Biblical Choleric

The Apostle Paul had no small degree of Choleric temperament. He was a prime persecutor of the early church, "Breathing threats and murder" (Acts 9:1) – before he was saved. He later pushed himself relentlessly until he had preached the Gospel around the then-known world. Who but a Choleric would crawl out from under a rock pile and the next day walk twelve miles to preach the gospel? Yet when filled with the Holy Spirit, Paul exhibited a gentleness and compassion that was contrary to his natural temperament. Yes, the Holy Spirit can control even Cholerics, who seem to find it hardest to realize what Christ meant when he said, "Without Me you can do nothing" (John 15:5). There is no limit to what the Choleric can do when he learns to walk in the Spirit and to abide in Christ.

Now I would like to have you meet the third temperament type . . .

Maestro Melancholy

Maestro Melancholy is often referred to as the "black" or "dark" temperament. Actually he is the richest of all the temperaments, for he is an analytical, self-sacrificing, gifted, perfectionist type, with a very sensitive emotional nature. No one gets more enjoyment from the fine arts than the Melancholy.

By nature Maestro is prone to be an introvert, but since his feelings predominate, he is given over to a variety of moods. Sometimes his moods will lift him to heights of ecstasy that cause him to act more extrovertish. However, at other times he will be gloomy and depressed; during these periods he is withdrawn and can be quite antagonistic.

Maestro Melancholy is a very faithful friend, but, unlike the Sanguine, he does not make friends easily. He will not push himself forward to meet people but lets people come to him. He is perhaps the most dependable of all the temperaments, for his perfectionist tendencies do not permit him to be a shirker or let others down. His natural reticence to put himself forward is not an indication that he doesn't like people. He not only likes others, but he also has a strong desire to be loved by them. Since disappointing experiences make him reluctant to take people at face value, he is prone to be suspicious when others seek him out or shower him with attention.

His exceptional analytical ability causes him to diagnose accurately the obstacles and dangers of any project he has a part in planning. This is in sharp contrast to the Choleric, who rarely anticipates problems or difficulties but is confident he is able to cope with whatever problems arise. This characteristic often finds the Melancholy reticent to initiate some new project or in conflict with those who wish to. Occasionally, when he is in one of his great moods of inspiration, he may produce some great work of art or genius. These accomplishments are often followed by periods of great depression.

Melancholies usually find their greatest meaning in life through personal sacrifice. They seem to have a desire to make themselves suffer and will often choose a difficult life vocation, involving great personal sacrifice. They tend to be very thorough and persistent in their pursuit of a chosen goal, and they are more likely to accomplish great good.

As a general rule, no other temperament has a higher IQ or more creativity or imagination than a Melancholy, and no one else is as capable of such high-quality "perfect" work.

Habits of temperament

When Melancholy motorists leave home, they've prepared for the trip well in advance. They study the map and know the best route from A to Z. Of all the temperaments, they are the most likely to keep a complete log of their driving history, including gas and oil consumption and car repairs. Legalists by nature, they rarely speed and may even drive one mile under the speed limit in the left-hand lane of the freeway, with sadistic glee forcing faster drivers to jockey through traffic to pass them. If they get a ticket, it is usually for refusing to yield the left lane to faster-moving traffic. At this point these Melancholys' reaction is one of great indignation. After all, weren't they observing the speed limit?

As for the yard, Maestro Melancholy has a natural aptitude for growing things and usually maintains the best yard in the neighborhood. He is one who talks to and babies his plants, and on almost any weekend you'll find him on hands and knees, "manicuring" his lawn and hedges.

Melancholies are very picky eaters. It takes them forever to make up their minds about what to order, but once their food arrives they savor every bite.

The checkbook? Melancholies usually put everything on a computer, keep a rigid budget, and know exactly what everything cost them and whether it has been profitable.

Career bests

Most of the world's great composers, artists, musicians, inventors, philosophers, theoreticians, theologians, scientists, and dedicated educators have been predominantly Melancholies. Name a famous artist, composer, or orchestra leader, and you have identified another genius (and often eccentric) Melancholy. Consider Rembrandt, Van Gogh, Beethoven, Mozart, Wagner, and a host of others.

Almost every true musician has some Melancholy temperament, whether he is a composer, choral conductor, performing artist, or soloist. This often accounts for the Melancholy's lament that seems to find its way into so much of our music – both in and out of the church. Just yesterday my wife and I were driving to the airport when a country-western tune was crooned (or warbled, depending on your point of view) over the radio. We looked at each other and laughed as the wail of the Melancholy was so apparent – and that song is one of today's top tunes.

The influence of temperament on a person's musical ability was apparent several years ago as our church evaluated a gifted minister of music and his piano-playing wife, obviously a Choleric. On the way home I remarked to my wife that I couldn't understand how a Choleric could be such a good pianist. Beverly replied, "She is a mechanical musician – by strong willpower she forced herself to learn to play the piano well, but she doesn't feel her music." As it turned out, the fantastic arrangement she used that night had been written by her husband, a Melancholy. Although he was not a pianist, he could "feel" music.

One vocation that seems to attract the Melancholy, surprisingly enough, is acting, even though we tend to identify this profession with extroverts. On stage the Melancholy can adopt another personality, no matter how much extroversion it requires, but as soon as the play is over, he reverts back to his own more introvertish personality.

All Melancholies, of course, do not enter the professions or arts, many become craftsmen of high quality – finish carpenters, bricklayers, plumbers, plasterers, scientists, horticulturalists, mechanics, engineers, and members of almost every profession that provide a meaningful service to humanity.

Almost any humanitarian vocation will attract Melancholies to its staff. For years I have watched doctors, and almost every doctor I know is either predominantly or at least secondarily a Melancholy. It would almost require a Melancholy's mind to get through the rigors of medical school, for a doctor has to be a perfectionist, an analytical specialist, and a humanitarian propelled by a heart that yearns to help other people.

Any vocation that requires perfection, self-sacrifice, and creativity is open to Melancholies. But they tend to place self-imposed limitations on their potential by underestimating themselves and exaggerating obstacles.

In the building trades, the Melancholy may want to supervise construction. But he would be better off hiring a project supervisor who works better with people – and then spend his own time on the drawing board. He becomes frustrated by ordinary personnel problems and, with his unrealistic perfectionist demands, adds to them.

Biblical Melancholies

No temperament has a much natural potential when energized by the Holy Spirit as the Melancholy. Many outstanding Bible characters had strong Melancholy tendencies; all the prophets were Melancholy, as was Solomon and the Apostle John.

And then there was Moses – a gifted introvert filled with self-doubt who eventually trusted God to make him one of the greatest leaders in all history. Yet Moses never had victory over his anger, which limited God's use of his life and resulted in his dying without entering the Promised Land.

Now I would have you examine the fourth temperament type . . .

Flip Phlegmatic

Flip Phlegmatic gets his name from what Hippocrates thought was the body fluid that produced a calm, cool, slow easygoing, well-balanced temperament. Life for Flip is a happy, unexcited, pleasant experience in which he avoids as much involvement as possible.

Calm, easygoing Flip Phlegmatic never seems to get ruffled, no matter what the circumstances. He has a very high boiling point and seldom explodes in anger or laughter but keeps his emotions under control. This is the one temperament type that is consistent every time you see this person. You see, Flip Phlegmatic is usually kindhearted and sympathetic but seldom conveys his true feelings. He feels much more emotion than appears on the surface and has a good capacity to appreciate the fine arts and the "finer things" of life.

Phlegmatics do not lack for friends because they enjoy people and have a naturally dry sense of humor that others enjoy. These people can have a crowd "in stitches" and never crack a smile. They have the unique capability of seeing something humorous in others and the things they do. They have a retentive mind and are often quite capable of being good imitators.

One of their great sources of delight is needling or poking fun at the other temperament types. They are annoyed by – and often confront – the aimless, restless enthusiasm of the Sanguine. They are disgusted by – and prone to ridicule – the gloomy moods of the Melancholy. They take great delight in throwing ice water on the bubbling plans and ambitions of the Choleric.

Phlegmatics tend to be spectators in life, and they try not to get too involved with the activities of others. In fact, it is difficult for them to be motivated to move beyond their daily routine. This does not mean that they cannot appreciate the need for action and the difficulties of others. A Phlegmatic and a Choleric may see the same social injustice, but the two will have entirely different responses. The crusading spirit of the Choleric will cause him to say, "Let's get a committee organized and campaign to do something about this!" The Phlegmatic would be more likely to respond, "These conditions are terrible! Why doesn't someone do something about this?"

But beneath the cool, reticent, almost timid Phlegmatic is a very capable combination of abilities. When once aroused to action, he proves to be a most competent and efficient person. Phlegmatics tend not to take leadership on their own, but when it is thrust upon them, they can be good leaders. I've labeled them "reluctant leaders."

Secretly, a Phlegmatic may aspire for a promotion on the job, but it would be against his nature to volunteer. Instead, he may patiently wait until more discordant and inept personalities make a mess out of things and then assume the responsibility only after it is forced upon him. Unfortunately, in many instances Phlegmatics wait their lives away and opportunity never knocks – because, although employers appreciate their capabilities, they don't envision them as leaders. Consequently, both the company and the employees lose.

The world has benefited greatly from the gracious nature of Phlegmatics. They have a conciliating effect on others and are natural peacemakers. In their quiet way, they have proven to be fulfillers of the dreams of others. They are masters at anything that requires meticulous patience and daily routine.

Habits of temperament

Flip Phlegmatic is the slowest driver of all. The last one to leave an intersection, he rarely changes lanes and is an indecisive danger when joining the flow of freeway traffic from an entrance ramp. He invariably stops when he should be moving with the flow of traffic. He is a poky "Sunday driver" seven days a week. He gets few tickets and rarely has accidents – but he can be a road hazard.

The Phlegmatic's lawn usually suggests that its owner is still in the house late Saturday morning, sipping his third cup of coffee – because he is. Capable of superior lawn care, Flip will scrupulously attend to "the old plantation" because his desire to rest is overcome by his drive to do the accepted thing. Much depends, of course, on whether he has been taking Geritol and wheat germ regularly.

Phlegmatics are the most deliberate eaters of all and are invariably the last ones finished. That is the main reason they rarely gain weight. Weight specialists advise obese patients to eat slowly, for it takes twenty minutes for food passing into the mouth to shut off hunger pangs.

Again, the checkbook: Phlegmatics are accurate bookkeepers, keep excellent records, and are able to balance to the penny.

Career bests

Phlegmatics seem drawn to the field of education. Most elementary school teachers are Phlegmatic. Who but a Phlegmatic could have the patience necessary to teach a group of first graders to read? A Sanguine would spend the entire class period telling stories to the children. A Melancholy would so criticize them that they would be afraid to read aloud. And I can't even imagine a Choleric as a first grade teacher – the students would leap out the windows! The gentle nature of the Phlegmatic assures the ideal atmosphere for such learning. This is not only true on the elementary level but in both high school and college, particularly in math, physics, grammar, literature, and languages. It is not uncommon to find Phlegmatics as school administrators, librarians, counselors, and college department heads.

Another field that appeals to Phlegmatics is engineering. Attracted to planning and calculation, they make good structural engineers, sanitation experts, chemical engineers, draftsmen, mechanical and civil engineers, and statisticians. Most Phlegmatics have excellent mechanical aptitude, making good mechanics, tool-and-die specialists, craftsmen, carpenters, electricians, plasterers, glassblowers, and watch and camera repairers.

Currently the biggest problem faced by industry pertains to personnel. With wages for many jobs skyrocketing, disharmony in a department can so demotivate employees that the employer may lose millions of dollars in productivity. In recent years management has discovered that experienced Phlegmatics often make excellent foremen, supervisors, and managers. Because they are diplomatic and unabrasive, they work well with people. When given positions of leadership, they seem to bring order out of chaos and produce a working harmony conducive to increased productivity. They are well organized, never come to a meeting unprepared or late, tend to work well under pressure, and are extremely dependable.

Phlegmatics are definitely not risk takers. They often stay with one company for their entire working career.

Rarely do Phlegmatics either live up to their full capabilities or fail in life. Because they tend to struggle with the problem of personal insecurity, they may take a job with retirement or security benefits in mind. Therefore, civil service, the military, local government, or some other "good security risk" will attract them. Rarely will they launch out on a business venture of their own, although they are eminently qualified to do so. Instead, they usually enhance the earning power of someone else and are quite content with a simple lifestyle.

Biblical Phlegmatic

Abraham is a good example of a Phlegmatic. He is a classic example of how God can transform a person's natural weakness into a strength. Abraham's fear, worry, and indecision became resolution, courage, and action to the point that more space is given to Abraham in the New Testament than any other Old Testament character.

Comparing Two Work Environments

Recently I had an experience that graphically portrayed the differences of temperament. While speaking at a summer camp for high school students, I needed to go out and find a fax machine. In the small town nearby, the only fax available was in the education center. When I arrived by appointment, I found nine people hard at work. The calm, orderly, and efficient surroundings made me realize that this environment was peopled predominantly by Melancholies or Phlegmatics.

This was later confirmed when the superintendent carefully computed my bill and refused to take my money because it was against the rules.

Instead, he took me to the meticulous treasurer, who took me to the bookkeeper, who in turn relayed me to the cashier, who finally arranged for me to give my $1.44 to the switchboard operator, who kept the petty cash. The clincher was the petty cash box, which clearly revealed the touch of the perfectionist. Her change had been carefully stacked in neat piles of quarters, dimes, and nickels.

As I surveyed the environment and noted the employees' calm but definite concern for this minor problem, I silently laughed, remembering the scene of another office – the sales office where I bought an overhead projector. There the sales staff, chief executive, and all the employees were predominantly of the extrovertish Choleric or Sanguine temperaments. The place was a disorganized mess! Papers strewn everywhere, telephones and desks unattended, the office was a hubbub of noisy activity.

Finally, above the din of voices I heard the sales manager say to the staff, with a look of desperation, "One of these days we are going to get organized around here!" These two scenes show the natural contrast of the inherited traits that produce human temperament.

They also point out the fact that all four of the basic temperaments are needed to give variety and purposefulness in this world.

Now that you have met the four temperaments, you no doubt realize why "people are individuals." Not only are there four distinct types of temperaments that produce these differences, but the combinations, mixtures, and degrees of temperament multiply the possible differences. In spite of that, however, most people reveal a pattern of behavior that indicates they lean toward one basic temperament.

5

"I trusted only in myself to save me from others."

Broken from pride

Meet Annette . . .

When I made up my mind to do something I completely ignored all other reasoning and exhausted myself proving my point.

One of my greatest weaknesses growing up was my stubbornness and determination to do things my way.

How God would use and transform this stubbornness and pride would only be through the life changes that only come from great pain that result from my own trial and errors. Because I'd gotten saved at an early age of 9 years old, this stubbornness came through as I tried to save everyone else, but first I had to tell them how horrible they were. **I'd known what it felt like to be ridiculed in school for being overweight** and was also perceived as dumb because English was my second language and I struggled to hide it. Therefore, I allowed the hurt and anger to further my sense of pride. Even though I knew the living God who had saved my soul, I trusted only in myself to save me from others and their thoughts of me. It has only been through recent brokenness that God has used this weakness of stubbornness and determination to keep me on my knees resulting in the most incredible humbleness as I've had to trust only in Him–only because He's all I have left to trust. Isn't it funny how He allows circumstances to bring us to the end of ourselves?

Through my desperate prayers and with the same stubbornness I have had to fix things, I'm learning to submit all authority and control to Him. I'm determined to no longer be controlled or obsessed by my requests and needs. I know by faith that My Father has heard me, He

5

loves me, He is not punishing me by making me wait for the answer; He is my Answer and I will trust Him and NO ONE can make me do any different!

I'm so thankful that through life's storms He's changing me by using how He's made me to be a display of His splendor and glory. As I trust Him, I will reflect Him, if I determine to. **I am being broken from my self-reliance,** or pride, as He continually allows me to fail in my own attempts to make things happen or change people.

Recently, the Holy Spirit reminded me of a time several years ago when I totally lost my temper with my oldest child, who at the time was 12 years old. I'd bought him an expensive necklace and he'd broken it. I yelled at him about being irresponsible and throwing away so much money. At the time, I didn't realize that I'd made him feel less important than the necklace and money. He is now 17 years old and when the Lord asked me to call him and ask him to forgive me, at first, he didn't remember the incident. Through humble tears, it opened the door to tell him how much more important he is to me than any necklace could ever be–no matter the cost. Things will break, and He will continue to break them–I have no control over this, but I do have control over the love I show to my children. Through my love for them, they will know their Father's love and that it has no conditions. Although, I may never be completely stripped as Job or know the persecution of Paul, my complete desire is to be still totally surrendered and submitted to His Sovereignty and His plan. As I continue to walk and fall, I know He will be faithful to keep changing me to that place of complete trust in Him.

Stubborn, Determined, and Trusting
– Annette
Married with three children
Accounting Assistant
38

What Is Your "Message"?

Chapter Six

Now that you've gained understanding about your unique personality, let's look at another part of you.

I want you to look at your life experiences not in a self-pity manner or in a manner that brings disappointment or shame but from the standpoint of turning all your past experiences into hope for someone else ... in other words, your own, unique message.

You've been through something that somebody else is going through right now and they need **your** wisdom. They need to know what you know.

Most people think the greatest tragedy in life is death. The greatest tragedy in life is to live and not know your purpose.
– Myles Monroe

We've all had our share of adversity and we will continue to face adversity but adversity has a way of bringing out the champion that is on the inside of you.

Free to be yourself

A few years ago, I was ministering at Brother Oral Roberts' ministerial conference in Tulsa and after my session, Happy Caldwell, Myles Monroe, and myself went to lunch together. Myles is a brilliant guy. He is one of those guys who is so full of wisdom that you want to write down everything he says. So, we were having lunch and we started talking about purpose and plans and fulfilling the plan of God on our lives. Myles Monroe made this statement and it's so powerful that I wanted to share it in this book. He said, "Most people think the greatest tragedy in life is death. It's not." He said, "The greatest tragedy in life is to live and never know your purpose."

Having lived your whole life and never really having that assurance that you have accomplished or you've done what you were put on this planet to do, is a discouraging thought. So if you're saying, "I don't have any dreams, I don't have any plans, I don't have any goals," then obviously you desperately need to spend some time with God. You desperately need to make that a priority in your life. I've had people say, "Okay, Jerry, I agree with all that. I'm willing to do all that. But I know I'm not called to preach so how do I know what I am called to do?"

That's a valid question. Not everyone in the world is called to preach behind a pulpit. However, we are all called to minister in our everyday lives. I know many men and women who are not ordained ministers but have a powerful "ministry."

Some people are called and anointed to be successful, wealthy entrepreneurs. They have great influence in the business world and their success grabs the ear of the nonbeliever. They have an "audience" wanting to hear, "How do you do it?" They can minister on the job.

It's the same with the housewife and mother who has peace amidst all of her demanding responsibilities, her marriage is healthy and she enjoys her life. "How?" People want to know. "Why do you always have a smile?"

No matter what you do as a career or calling, God wants to use you to impact the people around you. He wants to use your personality, your style, and your experiences to help someone else.

"How do I know what my message is? I don't really have a message," you may be saying.

Let me help you by sharing with you how I discovered my message.

"I'll show them!"

Before I surrendered my life to the Lord in 1969, I was a quitter. I quit everything. If anybody made me mad, I'd quit! And it didn't take much to make me mad. I was looking for opportunities to quit. If the least amount of pressure was applied, I would just quit! And I didn't even realize this was a pattern in my life until I began to study the Word of God.

When Carolyn and I first married, I think I went through about six different jobs in a matter of six months! I would let the tailgate of my truck down when I arrived at work just in case I decided to quit before the day was up, then I could pack up all my tools in just a matter of minutes! Isn't that terrible? I had every kind of job, nothing made me happy, the conditions of each job made me mad and basically, I was just a miserable human being running from God and quitting everything I tried. I had no focus, no drive, no ambition other than owning my own paint and body shop but even that looked so impossible. My track record with jobs was not very impressive!

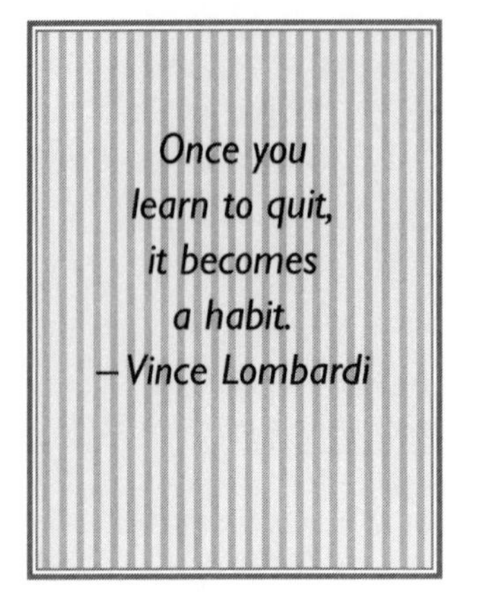

I remember Carolyn and I were eating dinner one night and she looked at me across the table and said, "So, where did you work today?" She couldn't even keep up with my new jobs! So, how did all that change in my life?

It wasn't until I completely surrendered my life to the Lord in 1969 and raised both hands to heaven and said, "Lord, I'm a failure. I've failed at everything I've done. I'm a quitter. What in the world would You want with me?" And I will never forget what I heard Him say because it changed my life forever. He said, "Don't worry about it, son. I am a Master at making champions out of failures!"

As I began to read the Bible and study different verses, there was one verse and one word that just popped off the page and into my heart and I finally realized, "That's it. That's my problem!"

. . . If ye continue in my Word, then are ye my disciples indeed; And ye shall know the truth, and the truth shall make you free.

John 8:31-32

That word ***continue*** got as big as the page in my Bible. I mean, it jumped off that page and my eyes got so big when I looked at the word. I thought, "That's it. I've never *continued* in anything. I've always quit." I discovered the word ***continue*** means *to carry on, go on, persist, keep on, prolong, maintain, go on with, remain, stay and last.* I wasn't doing any of those things.

That's when I made a quality decision that serving God was not going to be like everything else that I had tried. I was going to serve Him forever. I would not quit. I determined that "quitting" was no longer a part of my character or a pattern in my life anymore. I was going to develop the art of *continuing* in everything I set my hand to. I also knew that to change a pattern that had been developed for years in my life, it would take more than just willpower and discipline. It would take the anointing of God and building my spirit up daily by hearing and hearing the Word of God.

Your life's assignment is not your decision but your discovery.
– Mike Murdock

Was it easy? No. But I was determined. I had reached a point of being fed up with failing. I was finally able to trace my failures back to the fact that I was a good starter but I was a lousy finisher. I discovered that if I ever wanted to have success in any area of my life (as a husband, a father, a businessman, a child of God), I would have to stop quitting and determine to "continue."

So, what has my message been for over thirty-six years? **DON'T QUIT!**

I told my staff not too long ago that my message and my mandate has been to **talk people into winning!** In other words, don't quit! You can do it. Hang in there. Don't give up! It's not over. Your victory is just around the corner **if you won't give up!**

Isn't it amazing that God would anoint **me,** the former quitter, to preach messages of victory and winning? It's not ironic. It's not a coincidence. It's my story. I'm preaching from experience. I'm just telling my life every time I preach. It's real to me. I could relate to quitting (in the past) but not anymore. I didn't set out to preach these types of messages, but they just come natural to me. It just pours out of my spirit. No matter what topic the Lord puts in my heart to share whether it's in the area of finances, renewing your mind, forgiveness, tithing, etc . . . before the end of the message, I will have endeavored to talk people into winning and not quitting!

Your message is your life. Your message is what you've experienced; what comes natural to you. The most anointed sermons are the ones that people have firsthand experience along with revelation knowledge. I have revelation knowledge about "continuing" – it's not something I heard someone else preach and thought, *I'll try that!* No, it's real to me.

So, what is your story? What have you overcome or are you overcoming right now? Take note. Someone else is going through the same things, I can assure you. And they need to know what God is showing you about how to overcome it. They need your God-inspired message to get through it and come out a winner!

Least likely

Let's take a look at an example of a man who, in the eyes of most, was a nobody, but in the eyes of God was a champion.

God instructed Samuel to go and anoint the next king of Israel. He went to Jessie's house. He told Jessie to bring out all of his sons so he could look at them because one of them would be the next king of Israel. Samuel was being led by the Spirit of God as to who he was to anoint as the next king. Jessie brought out all of his sons except one, the nobody, the little insignificant one, the one that nobody would have thought could be king. He was just a sheepherder, a young boy, named David.

But the Lord said unto Samuel, Look not on his countenance, or on the height of his stature; because I have refused him: ***for the Lord seeth not as man seeth;*** *for man looketh on the outward appearance, but the Lord looketh on the heart.*

I Samuel 16:7

Boy, I'm glad God doesn't look on the height of our stature or I wouldn't have been called!

Look not on his countenance, or his stature (talking about one of the other boys who *looked* qualified). He looked like he should be *the one.* He was tall, big, and strong.

God never looks on the outward appearance, He sees what's on the inside. Men look on the outward appearance, they say, "You don't qualify. You'll never make it. That could never happen to you. How could you possibly have a message anyone could benefit from? After all, we know you!" That's exactly what Jesus' relatives thought of Him.

I'm glad it is not men who were responsible for my calling. It was God. I'm glad it's not men who determine whether you are anointed of God or not. It's God who determines that. So Samuel said to Jessie, "Are these all the boys you have?" Jessie said, "No. I have one more, but he doesn't amount to anything, he's a nobody" (Author's paraphrase).

Be careful when people start talking about other folks like they are nobodies. Watch those folks closely! They are just liable to turn into a champion. Notice, he finally brought David in. He was out herding the sheep, and you can imagine what he must have smelled like, and looked like.

Read what the next verse says,

Then Samuel took the horn of oil, and anointed him in the midst of his brethren . . .

I Samuel 16:13

Notice he didn't do it privately. He did it in front of all the others who, in the natural, were more qualified.

. . . and anointed him in the midst of his brethren: and the Spirit of the Lord came upon David from that day forward . . .

I Samuel 16:13

David was the least likely in the eyes of men, but not in the eyes of God. Remember this, it's not what men think that counts, it's what God thinks that counts. Samuel anointed him, declared him to be the future king of Israel, and don't you know that David's brothers were in shock? His entire family was in shock. They couldn't believe that ***he*** would be the one. The little nobody was going to become king!

So what if your family doesn't think these things can happen to you. So what if your friends laugh and persecute you. So what if they can't see what God sees. So what if there's never been any indication in your life that you are a potential champion. So what if you've failed at everything you've ever attempted in days past. If God says you are a champion, then you're a champion. If God says you can, then you can! If God says He wants to use your life to encourage others, then He will. Start seeing your life in light of the way God sees it. He wants to use your message in some way to help someone.

Overnight success?

Even though Samuel anointed David in the presence of his brothers and announced to them that this *little nobody* would become the future king of Israel, I want you to notice that it didn't happen overnight. In fact, as soon as the ceremony was over, David went right back to what he was doing. So even though you find out today or whenever it is you find it out, that God sees you as a champion and you have a message to tell, don't become discouraged because you don't become that champion overnight. In fact, you may go right back to what you were doing. You may go right back to that office, that plant, that shop, that place of business, that house, and nobody will be able to see any change. They won't be able to tell any difference at all.

David went right back with his sheep even though on the inside, there was a champion being born! And don't you know that after a period of time, his brothers began to mock him, "Oh, you're the king, huh? What are you the king of? A bunch of sheep? Champion, you call yourself a champion. Look at you out there with those smelly sheep" (Author's paraphrase).

You'll find that there's a lot of people who won't see what you see. That's the reason you have to learn to not be moved by what you see and not be moved by what you hear, and not be moved by what you feel. You can't be moved by what they say.

Some of my relatives thought I'd lost my ever-loving mind when they found out I was going to be a preacher. But now, when they are in need, they call the boy who lost his mind. Why? Because the *little nobody* has become a champion, hallelujah! Some of them still don't understand me, but they do understand this, when the boy prays, God moves.

So notice, it is not what men see, it's what God sees. Even though God may call you a champion, you may not become that champion in the next twenty-four hours. David went right back to his sheep. You read a little further and discover that when Saul called for him, where did they find David? Right where Samuel found him the first time ... with the sheep. But he didn't get discouraged. David was faithful. And if you'll be faithful to what the Word of God says and not allow others to distract you or discourage you, then the champion that's on the inside is going to come to the surface.

David had been anointed king in the presence of his brothers, but it took time before he became king. Even though he was king on the inside, it took a while to become king on the outside where everybody else could see it. Today you may be in debt up to your eyeballs, you may feel like the most miserable person in the world, you might not be able to remember the last time you succeeded at anything, but down on the inside of you, there is a champion ready to come out. So don't give up, don't be discouraged, don't quit. You're reading the right message for you.

Your message is still being developed

You may still be overcoming things from your past and you're actually walking toward your testimony right now. That's OK. Just keep walking. As I have previously stated, one of the greatest battles that many people have are with words that have been spoken over them by others. It grieves my spirit when I hear a mother or a father call a little child: "stupid" or say "You'll never amount to anything."

No weapon that is formed against thee shall prosper ...

Isaiah 54:17

What Is Your Message?

You have to remember that God's thoughts about you are good and not evil. He has planned a future for you, a bright future. He already knows how it's going to turn out and it's up to you to get in the flow of what God has already planned, so that your life matches the plan of God.

God orders the steps of good men and that means that He is always endeavoring to maneuver you into position to receive. If you will listen to Him, then you will always be in the right place at the right time and become the recipient of His blessing. That's the reason you need to be sensitive to His leadership. God's not trying to keep things from you, God's doing His utmost to get things to you!

God has always intended for you to live a blessed and a prosperous life. God has some extremely exciting things on the horizon for you. No matter how miserable your life may be at this very moment, God has a plan and God's plan is to turn your life around. If you won't run from Him, when you're distressed but run to Him, then He *can* and He *will* turn your captivity around. He says in His Word (Isaiah 65:24) that the moment you begin to cry out in prayer, the moment you begin to seek Him with all your heart, He will listen to you and He will begin the process of turning your life around. He's never at a loss to know what to do. God knows exactly what it will take to turn your life around. He's quite capable of turning every adversity in your life into victory!

And it shall come to pass, that before they call, I will answer; and while they are yet speaking, I will hear.

Isaiah 65:24

God's declaring that before you can utter the very first word of your prayer, He's already preparing a solution or a way out of your circumstances. While you are still calling on Him He's already involved in dispatching His angels to go forth and change your circumstances. Why? Because it's never God's will that you fail. It's never God's will that you stay in captivity, it's never God's will that you stay in bondage. God, apparently, is more interested in you being out of bondage than you are!

What stands between you and your destiny?

Now thanks be unto God which always causes us to triumph in Christ Jesus.
II Corinthians 2:14

Always! That's the will of God. It's never the will of God that you and I win a few – lose a few. God's will is that you triumph *always! Always triumph* is God's best for your life, no matter how impossible your circumstances look at this very moment. I don't care if you stumble and fall seven times, get up eight and go again! Don't accept defeat. Don't accept anything but triumph.

When I was a young boy, and playing baseball, in little league my coach told the team, "Boys, it's not whether you win or lose, it's how you play the game that counts." At eight years old, I didn't like the sound of that. I can remember walking away from him thinking, *That's the dumbest thing I've ever heard. It's not whether you win or lose? Well, why are we practicing every day?* I thought, *That's why we practice every day, so we'll win.*

As soon as my daddy would come home from work, I'd have his catcher's mitt waiting so I could pitch to him. Winning was everything! Now I realize he was probably referring to sportsmanship and how we conducted ourselves if we lost, but I learned not too long after that, that if you play the game right, you win! And it's certainly that way with God. If you play the game of life with God's rules, you always win. Now you may have setbacks from time to time, but I've also learned that setbacks are not final. Setbacks are not permanent. They are temporary. And they can become stepping stones to greater victories.

The true test to David's faithfulness and to holding onto what God had said to him was when he faced Goliath. Goliath represented a major obstacle that attempted to keep him from becoming what God said he would become. Goliath, just like our adversary, Satan, stood between David and his destiny.

Satan will stand between you and your destiny. He'll create barriers. He'll create obstacles, tests, and trials because he knows probably even better than some Christians that God has a wonderful future planned for you. He will stand between you and your destiny. He'll create every barrier he possibly can so that you will become discouraged and quit, and never fulfill what God has planned for you.

But I want you to notice that even though Goliath represented David's greatest obstacle to becoming what God said he would become, David chose to make Goliath a *stepping stone* instead a *stumbling block.*

The very adversity you're experiencing today, the thing that is trying to keep you from your destiny today, could become that stepping stone to your greatest victory! Your life experiences today will be your sermons tomorrow.

Goliath stood between David and his destiny, but David remained faithful. He believed that the God who was with him, this covenant-keeping

God, was able and willing to get him over and thank God, He did! He'll do the same for you if you'll just trust Him.

It's not how long you've been born again that will make you an effective witness. It's not necessarily the tremendous insight you have into God's Word that will make you an effective witness. You can start with what you know now; and what you know now is what Jesus of Nazareth has done in ***your life.*** That's your unique, personalized message that no one else can tell but ***you.***

Never get the idea that your testimony is no good because you weren't on drugs or because you hadn't made a horrible mess of your life before you met Jesus. I've heard people stand up and say, "I don't have a very good testimony. I've known Jesus all my life." That's a tremendous testimony! There are people who want to hear it. So you can start now with what Jesus has done in your life. But don't stop there. You also need to get into God's Word. You need to know the Word that supports what Jesus did in your life. People are looking for evidence. They want evidence, and you can give it to them by the Word of God and by your own testimony. That's what a witness is: one who provides evidence.

In addition to your personal experiences and challenges that you've overcome, I have found there's even more to your message than you think. I want to share with you six questions to ask yourself that will help you to discover your message.

#1. What are you most passionate about?

It could be that the very thing that you're most passionate about is something that God put in you. Now obviously, I'm not talking about things that are illegal, immoral, or sinful. If that's what you're most passionate about then you need to spend some more time with God. Passion is not a sinful thing when it is used properly. It can be used in a sinful way but passion is something that is God-given.

Many times, I hear people say the reason they got into a particular field of endeavor or they got into a particular profession and they were totally confident that was what God wanted them to do was first of all, because they realized they had a passion for it.

Passion, not obsession

Like I said, one of the activities I enjoy most is riding motorcycles. I've been riding motorcycles for as long as I can remember, and I enjoy them.

Now my motorcycle enjoyment has turned into the largest soul-winning outreach of Jerry Savelle Ministries. The Lord led me to start a Christian Bikers Club for other men and women who shared the same passion for God, for souls, and for motorcycles. We go on tours all over the United States (and other countries) and you ought to see the lives that come to Jesus simply because the motorcycles attracted them or caught their attention. We've had leaders of outlaw biker clubs come to our meetings and fall on their knees with tears pouring down their faces because they met Jesus for the first time.

God is using this passion that I have had ever since I was a young boy to draw people to Him. It's not a coincidence that I grew up on a race track and now the largest soul-winning event that our ministry hosts is at the Texas Motor Speedway!

God can use what you're passionate about as a "tool" to draw people to Him.

#2. What do you have a desire for?

The Bible says that if you delight yourself in the Lord, He will give you the desires of your heart. Desire is not a bad word. A lot of preachers have given the impression that if you have any kind of desire whatsoever, it's evil. Desire is a God-given thing.

Once again, do your desires line up with God's moral standard of living? If not, then spend some more time with God. Desires can be both Godly or ungodly. What is your greatest desire? What are you most passionate about? It could be that what you desire the most is what God is leading you to do with your life.

#3. What seems first nature to you?

What seems to come natural to you? It may be teaching, or working on automobiles, working with money, accounting, something that just comes natural to you. It could be a God-given gift. Don't rule that out. For the most part, those things that you're passionate about, those things that you seem to desire the greatest, or those things that seem to come natural to you, could perhaps be God's leading. God probably put that in you. It's all part of how God wants to use you.

#4. What do you do that seems to produce the best results?

Are there areas in your life where you apply yourself and you always get good results? Are you naturally gifted in sales? Do you enjoy being around people? Are you creative? What do you do that produces the best results? This could very well be a gift from God.

#5. What produces the greatest peace and happiness in your life?

The Bible says we are to follow peace. If something isn't producing peace in your life, then stop doing it. Make note of the times when you feel the greatest peace. The Bible says that God is the author of peace.

#6. What do you do that seems to bear witness with the Holy Ghost more than anything else?

Think about it. All of these can be indicators that you're on target. Perhaps those things were God-given, it's what God wants you to do and then it's just a matter of developing it and striving to be the best at it.

When I go to God in prayer, particularly when I need wisdom or direction, I write it in the form of a question first. I go to God with a Bible and a notebook and I write all the questions I have in my heart. I write them down. The reason I write them down is because I'm expecting answers. I am one of His sheep, I hear His voice, and He said He's laid up sound and Godly wisdom for the righteous, so I've made it a practice to always write my questions down. Write your questions down and then talk to God just like I'm talking to you.

If you don't get the answers the first time you go to prayer then refuse to quit. Keep a notebook by your bed stand so if you happen to hear something in your spirit just before you go to sleep or perhaps in the middle of the night, then you can write it down. Listen all the time for those answers. That's what I do and it has always worked.

You could go to God and say, "Father, the thing I'm most passionate about is singing. I have a great desire to sing. It seems to come natural to me. Is this what You want me to do with my life? Is this part of my calling and how you want me to share my message, my story, with others?" It could be very possible that it is God's gift and it's what He wants you to do. Once you sense that peace, then there's step one. If it seems to bear witness with you and the Holy Ghost, then go forward with it.

Say to God, "Now, I know that singing is a part of my life. Where do I go from here?" Continue to ask, "What are the next steps?" I found a scripture in Isaiah years ago when I was asking these questions about my ministry and it said "learn to do well." It was actually talking about shunning evil but that phrase "learn to do well," ministered to me. It means that you will never excel in anything you do if you don't learn to do it well. So study, research, and get around other people who do it well.

Whatever you do, do it well

In the automotive business, if I wanted to be the best, then I had to go to workshops. I had to get around people who knew what they were doing. I considered my dad as one of the best so I wanted to be taught by him. Sometimes the dealership would send me to seminars and workshops to learn more. What was I doing? Learning to do well. Years later, I wanted to do well in ministry. Kenneth Copeland had an "Excellence in Ministry Seminar" (his very first one) in his mother's basement in Fort Worth, Texas, and I went to it. He was showing me how to do well. I still apply those same principles today. What was God doing? He was honoring my desire to excel. He was honoring my desire to do well.

If you believe God's called you into the automotive business, or to be a singer, or an athlete, or a salesperson, or a preacher, then don't settle for just a job, determine that you're going to excel in it. Learn to do well and do whatever you have to do to research and study and become the best. Of course that is going to open doors to promotion.

I always go back to this rule about peace that I have. Did it produce peace or did it create confusion? If it creates confusion, then God didn't author it. If it creates peace, then God is behind it. That is a rule that has worked for me all these years.

Go. Go. Go.

Notice again Jesus' words:. . . *All power is given unto me in heaven and in earth. Go ye therefore . . .*

Matthew 28:18-19

Jesus is telling us that all power has been given to Him and that now He is giving it to us so we can go out and be witnesses for Him throughout the whole world.

You have a message. You also have an assignment. Don't keep your experiences with God to yourself. Share what you've learned with others. They need to hear what you know. Inspire others with your life.

You have a story to tell. You have a message of God's love, and God's healing power. Share it whenever you have an opportunity. Your story could have a profound impact on someone else.

Your background has everything to do with the God-given message which you have to inspire others.

For ye see your calling, brethren how that not many wise men after the flesh, not many mighty, not many noble, are called: God hath chosen the foolish things of the world to confound the wise; and God hath chosen the weak things of the world to confound the things which are mighty; And base things of the world, and things which are despised, hath God chosen, yea, and things which are not, to bring to nought things that are: That no flesh should glory in His presence.

I Corinthians 1:26-29

Free to be yourself

For [simply] consider your own call, brethren; not many [of you were considered to be] wise according to human estimates and standards, not many influential and powerful, not many of high and noble birth. [No] for God selected (deliberately chose) what in the world is foolish to put the wise to shame, and what the world calls weak to put strong to shame. And God also selected (deliberately chose) what in the world is lowborn . . .

I Corinthians 1:26-28 (Amplified)

God is not looking for those who have lived a so-called perfect life. There's nothing wrong with education, but God's not saying that you have to be an expert before He can use you. God's saying, *"Whatever the world says can't be used, I can use it."* Do you qualify yet? Whatever the world says there is absolutely no hope for, God sees a candidate. When your parents, your relatives, and your friends think that you will never amount to anything, God says, "There's one I can use . . ." So you qualify. You are a potential champion!

And God also selected (deliberately chose) what in the world is lowborn and insignificant and branded and treated with contempt, even the things that are nothing, that He might depose and bring to nothing the things that are, So that no mortal man should [have pretense for glorying and] boast in the presence of God.

I Corinthians 1:28-29 (Amplified)

God has chosen you and on the inside of you is unlimited potential! God is looking for people in these last days who will tap that potential and get maximum results with it.

Look at my friend Dennis Burke, one of the greatest teachers in the body of Christ today, and a man in whom I appreciate the anointing of God on his life. Would you believe that he used to be a long-haired, drug-addict, hippie, who does not even remember high school because he was in some other world while it was going on? That's hard to believe. If he hadn't said it, I wouldn't have believed it myself. Look at him now! He's a champion. His life is now a message.

Look at my friend Happy Caldwell. He was a liquor salesman. This man pastors one of the greatest churches in America today. He founded and pioneered the very first Christian television network in the state of Arkansas and he used to be a nobody! But look at him now! He's a champion. His life is a message that inspires others.

And I can't leave out my friend Jesse Duplantis! Can you believe that he was once a long-haired, rock-n-roller, get-down-with-his-bad-self, heathen-from-hell . . . a nobody, but God made a champion out of him! His life is a message.

Oral Roberts, a man who as a young boy, stuttered and was so embarrassed by it, that most people thought he'd never amount to anything. Satan fully intended to destroy his life but God . . . God looked down and saw a champion. Look what this man has accomplished in his lifetime. He has brought healing to his generation! His life is a message.

Look at the story of Kenneth and Gloria Copeland. They were nobodies and look what they have accomplished. They were boiling potatoes in a coffee pot because they had no stove, so far in debt they could hardly see straight and they've been pioneers in teaching God's covenant of prosperity for over four decades. Their lives are a message.

If you're a nobody now, then God wants to make a champion out of you if you will stand on His Word. Your life can be a message, too.

Free to be yourself

I was insignificant! I was just a little speck on planet earth wearing my "Jerry's Paint and Body Shop" uniform working on wrecked cars. I thought I was going to do that for the rest of my life! But God found this nobody out on North Market Avenue in a paint and body shop and said, "You know I believe I can use that nobody!" Now, my life is my message.

It is time for you to get over your past. It is time for you to get over what everybody has been saying about you. It is time for you to get over all the negative words that have been spoken over you! It is time for you to get over all of your previous mistakes! It is time for you to get over all your past failures! God says that He can use you. He needs you. He wants you. You're a champion! And you have a message to share with others. It's the story of your life.

The very challenges that we think are going to destroy us, God turns into a message of hope and deliverance for others.

So, what has my message been for over thirty-six years to millions of lives all over the world? Don't quit! My message is to talk people into winning. Doesn't God have a sense of humor?

What is <u>your</u> message? Think about it. Write it down.

6

"I felt trapped and unable to communicate with people."

From shy and timid to a voice of influence

Meet Delaina . . .

As a child, I was a very shy and timid little girl. My mind would be filled with words to say, but I could not speak them out verbally. I felt trapped and unable to communicate with people. Friends are very important to a child's development with social skills and mine were nonexistent. The few friends that I did have were invaluable to me.

One particular Sunday morning in Sunday school, my teacher told us stories about embarrassing moments and self-esteem. She explained about how God saw us as his beautiful, perfect creation and we were made in His image. At the age of 9 years old, I first heard about God's love for children and how proud He is of His creations. I cannot thank Mrs. Janice Nelon enough for that lesson that day. She shared about a life full of promise and exciting times to come. This simple Sunday school lesson changed a life forever.

I decided to unlock my mouth and trust that people would want to hear me.

My personality was transformed. I was friendly, fun-loving, energetic, and happy. My friends increased dramatically and I am still close to many of them today. God's timing is perfect in everything. As a teen, I could enjoy all the fun and friendships that develop during that stage of growth. Today, I enjoy meeting new people every day in my profession as a personal banker and volunteering at a Pregnancy Aid Center.

God changed me into a person with a voice that He can use to influence others to make the life-changing decision to follow Christ.

– Delaina
Married with two children
Personal Banker
45

Who Is Your Audience?

Chapter Seven

Audience? You might be wondering what I mean by that. You could be saying, *I don't have an "audience." I'm a housewife.* Or *I'm an accountant. I don't minister behind a pulpit.* Or, on the other hand, you could be in full-time ministry and you've never given thought to who your audience is.

When I say audience, I'm referring to the people who are drawn to you. What type of people are naturally drawn to you and you are drawn to them? These are the types of personalities and people that you feel most comfortable around, those with whom you "click."

It could be that you have something in common: backgrounds, hobbies, sports, children, careers, etc. It is interesting when you actually take a look at the people who have impacted your life the most and notice that there is probably something about them that you relate to.

It seems that men who have an interest in motorcycles and cars are naturally drawn to my ministry. I can't tell you how many people have come up to me and said, "When I heard you give your testimony of how you grew up on a racetrack and worked on old cars, that could have just as well been me up there . . . that's my story."

Immediately, there's a connection. Many women have told me that their husbands refused to go to church with them, but for some reason, they'll come to listen to me preach. Why? Because they relate to my life. And most of the time, it's because of my background.

I've told my wife for years that I'm the "blue collar preacher." The majority of my audience are the blue collar workers. Why? Because that's who I was before I surrendered my life to the Lord. I was in debt, my marriage was falling apart, my business was failing, I was beating on fenders, coming home with grease from head to toe, but I dared to pick up the Bible and believe that God could do something with me. And He did. My story is simply, "If God can do it for me, He can do it for you."

I've also recognized that many of the people who are drawn to this ministry are now successful businessmen and women but they used to be just like me. They were failing but they took the Bible and applied it to their life and turned a pattern of failing into success.

Many times, you'll discover that your audience, or the people who are most likely to listen to what you have to say, are people who are in the same condition you were in before you gave your life to the Lord or they are encountering the same challenges you've overcome in life.

Many people who have overcome obesity and overeating are now encouraging others who are challenged with their weight. How? Through their testimony. They are naturally drawn to and have compassion for the person struggling with weight. That's who their audience is.

Some are drawn to the outcasts and the insecure. Why? Because they once were insecure and felt rejected, but now they know who they are in Christ.

Most of the ministers who preach prosperity used to be poor and some even lived a poverty-stricken life for many years. Who comes to hear them preach? Those who need help with their finances. That's who their audience is most of the time.

What is your story?

And every one that was in distress, and every one that was in debt, and every one that was discontented, gathered themselves unto him . . .

I Samuel 22:2

These people were David's "audience." *. . . he became a captain over them: and there were with him about four hundred men . . .*

I Samuel 22:2

David attracted 400 people who were in distress, who were in debt and who were discontented. Now what in the world are you going to accomplish with 400 people who are distressed, in debt, and discontented? If you study this out, you'll find that this same group of people, eventually became the mighty men of David! The mightiest warriors in all of Israel, were nobodies when David met them. Well, who was David before he became king of Israel? A nobody. A little shepherd boy with no future.

Was David ever distressed or discontented? Read the Psalms. They are full of his writings about the stress he was under, the pain in his soul, and his desire to just run away. But what happened? David would always encourage himself in the Lord. Eventually, God would use him to encourage others who were just like him: distressed, discontent, and in debt . . . wanting to just run from it all. God used his experiences in life to be his message to help other "David's" who were going through the same things he went through. Your audience is predominantly people who are going through similar situations you've gone through. They can relate to you.

The word ***distressed*** in the literal Hebrew is translated: *Under great pressure, under great stress.* Many of you who are reading this book are under great pressure and under great stress. Well, I've got a good report for you: you are a potential winner!

And anyone who was ***in debt,*** is translated as *having so many creditors that there was no way to pay them off.* Are you like that? Have you got so many debts that there is no way to pay them all? Then you are a potential winner!

Discontented means they had been wounded in their spirit, and in their soul. They had been rejected, ridiculed, and hurt. They were wounded people!

I remember hearing someone say to Oral Roberts many years ago: "Brother Roberts, your partners are the same kind of people that David attracted." The kind of people that his ministry attracted were the ones the world considered nobodies. Pentecostal people back then, as far as the religious world was concerned, were *nobodies.* The unlearned, the ignorant, the nobodies, and that's who Oral Roberts' ministry attracted the most. And those "unlearned, ignorant, nobodies" built a University. The only Holy Ghost inspired, University in America today. *Nobodies* built it. And that's the kind of people that David attracted. When other folks know that you were a nobody, and they see what God has done in your life, then suddenly they want to be around you. Because if God can do it for you, then He can do it for them.

Think about your life. Think about specific things you've had to overcome. Go back as far as childhood and think of detailed accounts when you had challenges, pains, trials, and temptations. Instead of remembering all your mistakes, think of how you overcame them.

What did you do?

You obviously didn't throw in the towel because you're still here. So, what did you do? Tell your story. Let God use you. I'm not saying you have to reveal every detail of your past but just let the Lord instruct you and guide you so you'll know what He wants you to share with hurting people.

You might say, "You don't understand the mistakes I've made." Use them to help others. You might say, "I was abused!" Use your testimony to help others who were abused. Since you know that the healing power of God can restore what Satan has stolen, tell others. They need to hear your story.

Make Jesus attractive

The Church realized that Christians shouldn't conform to the world however; in their zeal not to conform, they pushed nonconformity to the extreme. As a result of their one-sided view, they did not make the Gospel attractive. They actually gave the world a very distorted picture of what a Christian is supposed to look like and be like. They presented an image of poverty, ignorance, and fanaticism, which was as unappealing as it was untrue.

Such well-intentioned but sadly misinformed Christians have tried so hard not to draw attention to themselves that they now stick out like a sore thumb. Such extremism does not adorn the Gospel at all. It makes it look foolish and repugnant. In other words, we lost our audience.

As a reaction against this kind of negative presentation, many Christians have gone to the opposite extreme. They have gone to great lengths to adapt to the world's ways, and to imitate it. They are so afraid of appearing ignorant or fanatical or out of step with the times, they have adopted the world's values rather than remaining true to God. They care more about appearances than they do truth. In short, they are more concerned with respectability than they are with godliness.

But just because people go from one extreme to the other does not mean there is not a central truth. And that truth is that although we Christians are in the world, we are not of the world. While we are to go into all the world and present to it a positive, attractive Gospel, we are not to be influenced by the world. We are not to be conformed to the world, we are to conform to the image of Jesus Christ.

We should always strive to present to people, whatever their station in life, a pleasant and attractive image. We ought to make certain we do a good job of representing Christ so that others will be attracted to Him.

That does not mean that we should compromise our integrity or our Christian principles in an attempt to win the respect of others. There is a delicate balance to be maintained between fear of God and fear of man. Simply stated, we should always strive to maintain godliness, but in a way so as not to alienate ourselves from the very people who are in most need of that godliness.

Who Is Your Audience?

As Christians we are called to be fishers of men, but any fisherman can tell you that you catch fish with a *lure,* not a club. If we really want to reach people for Christ, we must present to them a Christ of love and forgiveness and compassion, one who cares for them and their needs. Present the truth of what God's love has done in your life . . . in your own words with your own personality.

The world is hurting today. People are suffering. Everything they have ever trusted in is falling apart right in front of their eyes. People are desperately seeking solutions for their problems, provision for their needs, direction for their lives, hope for their future, stability and power and peace. We Christians are supposed to have the key to all those things which the world needs and seeks. That key is a personal relationship with God through His Son, the Lord Jesus Christ.

But unless we are careful to give evidence of all those good things in our own lives, there is little reason to expect the world to want what we have. Especially if we assume a pious, holier-than-thou attitude and sit in judgment upon them. They need to know, in many cases, that ***you've been there.*** You understand. You used to be just like them but now you know the Truth. You have the answer and it's in a personal, intimate relationship with Jesus. People need to know you understand. Then, show them how God changed your life.

Be merciful to those who doubt; snatch others from the fire and save them; to others show mercy, mixed with fear – hating even the clothing stained by corrupted flesh.

Jude 22-23 (NIV)

Don't compromise what you believe. Don't compromise the Word of God. Make people wonder what you have that they don't have. Be courageous. Take a bold step in doing what God says to do.

Your "audience" may not be people who grew up just like you did, but it may be that they've dealt with the same insecurities you did or the same temptations or addictions.

Like I said, audience doesn't mean a crowd of people. I'm referring to the people in your office, the people at your child's soccer game, the person in the grocery store who just starts talking to you for no reason. There are people who are drawn to you because you have something they need and are crying out for and God wants to use you to give them hope for a better life . . . in Jesus.

With this in mind, don't ever again think of people you "bump into" or just happen to meet as a coincidence. Don't look at it casually. I like to think of them as *divine appointments.* It doesn't mean you have to start "testifying" to every person that says, "Hello." Make Jesus attractive by just being yourself and let the Holy Spirit lead you into discussions about what God's done in you and what He wants to do in them.

You know what they want to see: Reality. So, be yourself. That's more attractive than appearing superspiritual. That's why I can walk into a motorcycle shop, strike up a conversation with a total stranger about bikes and accessories, etc., and never mention that I'm a preacher. Instantly, we have something in common. But they can always tell there's something different about me. And that's what they want. I call those divine appointments.

Look at where you spend your time. Look at the people who seem to want to talk to you. Be yourself with them. Make them curious about why you seem joyful. And as the Lord directs, share the love of Jesus with them, always confirming that God loves them right now, just as they are. Then, take it from there. You have an audience. They need "your message." Don't run them off. Be sensitive and look for those divine appointments.

7

"I was stubborn as a mule."

Stubbornness changed to resolve

Meet Eric . . .

Very few people come to know Jesus Christ as their personal Savior without some sort of luggage and I was no exception. When I first became a Christian I easily conquered drugs, alcohol, and the things that many Christians overcame that were brought up in the '60s and '70s. **I had a problem that would prove to be much more difficult to conquer**. My major dysfunction as a young man was that I was stubborn. The root cause for most of the troubles I went through as a teen and in my early twenties was that I was stubborn as a mule.

I was an expert at being stubborn. I was brought up in a long lineage of extremely difficult people. "Stubborn" was "born" into a difficult family! As far as I can remember it started with my grandmother.

My grandmother traveled to California from Oklahoma back in the 1940s along with her husband and six children (you've seen the Grapes of Wrath)? Anyway, shortly thereafter my grandfather was killed in a construction accident. As you could imagine, life was not easy. She was probably a stubborn person already. This didn't help. I loved my grandmother, but you never knew whether she was a friend or foe. My father carried on many of the same characteristics my grandmother had.

I was a loser and lived in continual conflict.

My father was a hard-working person. He was in the military for twenty years. He never drank and taught us good morals. My mom went to church, he didn't. He was basically a good man. However, a major flaw in his personality was that he was stubborn. **When you are stubborn you live in conflict.** Being hardheaded didn't make him happy, or for that matter, anyone else around him. I love my father, and I thank the Lord that he finally got saved. Since then, he has changed dramatically and our fences have been mended.

As for myself, I also carried on many of the same characteristics. This caused me to blunder through the first few years of my adulthood. I didn't listen to my parents' advice. **I lived totally according to my soul and emotions.** I was an angry person and extremely stubborn. As an example, I was in the military and refused to make rank or, in civilian talk – go to a higher rank. They gave me extra duty, kept me on the ship. I still wouldn't budge. I got out of the navy as an E-2.

When I got saved, the Lord brought to my attention how thickheaded I was. Slowly I was able to overcome stubbornness. I love to learn from other people. When I have a difficult decision, I always get advice from people I consider wise. I love people and value others' opinions. The Lord has taken my stubbornness and has changed it to resolve. I'm not a pushover, but I love unity. I am a hearer and a doer. I have worked with teenagers for almost twenty years. I am a youth pastor and I have had a business for almost twenty years. Thank you, Jesus, for changing me. Thank You for making me strong.

– Eric
Married with two children
Youth Pastor/Self-employed
44

#1. A PLAN

If you've been inspired and motivated to be yourself and determined to do what God's called you to do and make a difference with your life, then you must have a plan. Nothing will just happen automatically. The primary reason why most people do not succeed is because they do not plan. Planning is a choice.

> *The poorest man is not without a cent, but without a dream.*
> *– Unknown*

Recently, we had our Chariots of Light Christian Biker Club tour in Florida. We took off from Fort Worth, Texas, and we ended up in Daytona Beach, Florida, at "Bike Week." There were approximately 350,000 bikers that showed up in Daytona for Bike Week. We had planned this tour for a long time, for months in advance. The Chapter

President in Miami was responsible for organizing the tour in that area including the routes we would take, what hotels we would stay in along the way, what churches we would minister in, and how long it would take to get to each city, etc.

When you have anywhere from 50 to 100 bikers all riding together, then you have to plan ahead. When you have that many bikers in convoy coming into a town, you have to have a thought-out plan. You even have to know ahead of time if there are restaurants along the way. Have you ever seen 100 bikers show up hungry? Someone has to go in advance of this tour and find out if there are restaurants that can handle 100 bikers. There was a lot of planning that had to take place. You don't just say, "Let's all go to Daytona Bike Week." Someone asks, "When do we meet?"

You've got to be careful if you don't know where you're going because you might not get there.
– Yogi Berra

"Anytime."

"Where?"

"Anywhere."

We will never get there. There has to be some planning.

Failing to plan is planning to fail

I've discovered that most people do a better job at planning a trip that will only last for a week than they do planning their life which is a lifetime. A lot of people do not succeed simply because they do not plan. God didn't just wake up one morning and say, "You know, I think I will make a universe." That is not the way God operates. Nothing God does is by coincidence. God is the Master Planner. As we've discussed earlier, He has a plan that He made for your life even before you were formed in your mother's womb. And God thoroughly planned the universe.

... and comprehended the dust of earth in a measure ...

Isaiah 40:12

The word ***comprehend*** means to *grasp mentally, to fully understand, to possess the ability to carry out to fruition.* In other words, before God ever created the universe he thought it out. He comprehended it. He planned for it. If you just read Genesis chapter 1 – *and in the beginning God said let there be ...*, then you might think God just got up one morning and said, "Let there be this and let there be that and hey, let's have this, too." That is not the way God did it.

The Lord by wisdom hath founded the earth; by understanding hath he established the heavens.

Proverbs 3:19

Notice wisdom, understanding, and comprehension were all a part of God creating the universe. In other words, He planned before He went into action. The reason so many people do not succeed today is because they have never made the choice to plan **first.** You know as well as I do that if you want to be a doctor, then you have to make plans to be a doctor. If you want to own your own business, then you have to make plans to own your own business, and if you want a better life, then you have to make plans for a better life. All of that is a choice.

So many people live for the moment. Whatever happens, happens.

What will be, will be. You are not going to experience God's best with that kind of attitude. It takes planning. Success in any endeavor requires planning and planning is a choice. If you never succeed at anything, it is simply because you didn't plan to succeed. Success doesn't come easy. If it did, everybody on the planet would be successful.

Recently, as I was flying back from Raleigh, North Carolina, I was watching my pilot. He had a plan. As a matter of fact, I won't get in an airplane with a pilot who does not plan. The first thing I want to see a pilot do is go over that checklist.

Pilots file a flight **plan.** Think about that. In other words, they know before they ever leave the ground what it is going to take to reach their destination. In fact, he can tell the people at the destination an approximate arrival time. He has already worked all that out. Even if we have to stop and refuel somewhere, he knows how long it is going to take.

Well, you know as well as I do that there are some stormy conditions that show up in life from time to time and you need a "flight plan." Planning, once again, is a choice. Life can be full of stormy conditions and that is why you need a plan. With a plan, you can maneuver through life's storms much easier, and that is what the Word of God is all about. It is God's plan for your life. It is your flight plan for this journey through life. Knowing what God says about your life puts you in a position of advantage. Not only that, but it puts you in position to take control of your destiny.

Without the knowledge of God's plan for your life, then you will remain locked into your present circumstances and your present surroundings. You will not be able to go any further because you have no knowledge of God's plan. That is why Paul prayed in Colossians 1:9 *... that ye might be filled with the knowledge of his will in all wisdom and spiritual understanding.*

God wants you to be filled with the knowledge of His will. Why? Because to know His will is to know His plan and when you know the plan of God, then once again you can maneuver through life's storms much easier.

If you believe that success belongs to you, then start planning to succeed. I want to challenge you to spend as much time as possible in the Word of God so that you will be filled with the knowledge of God's plan.

It is wonderful going to bed at night knowing that you are in the perfect will of God. It is awesome getting up in the morning knowing you are right where God wants you to be and that you are right on target with what God has called you to do.

You mean you can know that, Jerry?

Yes, you can, but it takes fellowship with Him. It takes time in His Word.

The art of setting goals

It is a proven fact that without setting goals it is not very likely that you will enjoy any high level of success. You might have a few successes here and there but it will not be a continual thing in your life if you never set goals. Until you learn how to set goals and until you learn how to persevere while you are waiting for them to become reality, then it is not likely that you will be successful. It will only be wishful thinking. A person who never sets goals is like a ship without a rudder and a ship without a rudder is like a person who just wanders aimlessly through life. There are a lot of people like that today.

As we've already shared throughout this book, your first goal, obviously, should be to discover what ***God*** wants you to do with your life. Once you become a Christian, then you have an inside track to God and now you can discover what God truly wants you to do with your life. That should be your first goal or your first pursuit. This is what the apostle Paul said when he met Jesus on the road to Damascus.

. . . Lord, what wilt thou have me to do?

Acts 9:6

He hadn't even been born again fifteen seconds and the first thing that came out of his mouth was, "What do you want me to do with my life?"

Prior to that time, Paul had been pursuing his own goals. He was one of the most educated men of his day. He was an intellect. He thought he was doing God a service by persecuting and having Christians put in prison and even stoned to death. Yet when he met Jesus, he realized that everything he had done up to that time was not what God really wanted him to do. His number one goal was to find out what God wanted.

Obviously, for you to find that out, it is going to take fellowship with God. It is going to take spending time with God on a **daily basis.** God has His ways. He is not going to lay it all out at one time. He is going to give you one step at a time and then He will expect you to walk by faith. Most people want step number ten before they even do step one. *Lord, if you will just lay out my whole life for me so I will know how it is going to turn out then I will walk by faith.*

Well, it would not take faith if you already knew how everything was going to turn out.

One step at a time

The first time I went to Africa all I knew was what I learned from men like Oral Roberts and T. L. Osborne. They had open-air crusades. Well that was all I knew. I watched their films. I studied their methods. I knew God wanted me to go to Africa so I thought that was what I should do. Step one: go to Africa. So I had crusades set up all over the country. The first crusade I did we had thousands of people show up that first night. It was awesome. My first time to ever be on African soil and I had thousands of people eager to hear the Word! When I gave the invitation to meet Jesus, hundreds came forward for salvation. It was awesome!

The next night, the crowds were bigger and the next night, more people came forward for salvation, but I noticed that a lot of the same people who came the first night for salvation came again. Then the third night, more of the same people who came the first night and the second night to get saved came forward again. I knew that T. L. Osborne had been in that same city just a short time ahead of me, so I asked my coordinators if they were in the T. L. Osborne meetings. They said they were. I asked them if they recognized any of the people who came forward to get saved in my meetings as people who had come forward for salvation in T. L. Osborne's meeting. They said, "Oh yes. Many of them did."

I thought, *This is not what God sent me here for. These people need to be discipled – they need to learn how to live by the Word of God.*

Step one was to get me to Africa. When I got there, I found out what I was doing was not really what God wanted me to do. He wanted me to teach. He wanted me to disciple. Let others evangelize them and then I will disciple them. Step one was just *do what I knew to do.* But once I got there, I realized God had other plans for me so I cancelled the remaining crusades and I began ministering to all the pastors. We had about eighty pastors show up. Now when you come back home and people ask, "How many people did you have in your crusade," and you say, "eighty!" That doesn't sound impressive. It sounds better to say 20,000. People are into numbers. But listen, if I can get eighty pastors grounded in the Word, then I can impact the whole nation. So I realized that step one was to get me to Africa. Step two was to find out what God wanted me to do once I got there and not what he wanted someone else to do. Then He began to lay it out as I took each step, and from there, we began to build churches. We eventually built nearly fifty churches and continued to train pastors. Yes, we did get into evangelism again, but we made sure we had a church in that area so we could disciple the people who were receiving salvation.

Vision comes in steps

God is not going to lay it all out at one time. It is one step at a time so don't get discouraged. The Bible says that the ***steps*** of *a good man,* (not the strides, not the leaps, not the jumps, but the steps) ***are ordered by the Lord*** (Psalm 37:23). I realize that steps are the slow way. We don't like steps. We like leaps. We want to run and jump and leap but steps are the way that God deals with your life – one step at a time.

So if you are going to discover what God wants you to do, then step one is going to demand that you spend time with Him. Once you discover what He wants you to do, then you have to ask yourself this question – **am I willing to pay the price?** Trust me . . . there is a price.

If you are determined to pay the price, if you are willing to stick with what God wants you to do, then He will help you achieve it. He will help you get the job done. God will not only reveal to you what He wants you to do, but He will also equip you with the ability to do it.

I can do all things through Christ which strengtheneth me.

Philippians 4:13

One of the most common weaknesses in most people is if their goals don't come to pass quickly, then they tend to stop believing that they can achieve them.

Most of the time your goals, your plans, your vision will look impossible. You realize, "Hey, I don't know if I can do this or not." That is the reason Paul said, "I can do ***all things through Christ***." In other words, you are not in this alone. You have the Greater One on the inside of you. He will not only reveal what He wants you to do but He will give you the ability to accomplish it.

. . . that we may boldly say, The Lord is my helper . . .

Hebrews 13:6

You can count on God to help you. You must never stop believing in your God-given ability to accomplish what most people consider the impossible. God sees you as a winner and you need to continue to see yourself as a winner. No matter how impossible your goals may seem, never give up on them. When you are single-minded, then there will always come a supernatural ability to accomplish those goals.

Sit down and begin setting goals, realistic goals, to get you started toward the plan of God for your life. What can you do now to prepare yourself? What books can you read? Which seminars can you attend? What is your plan of action? I encourage you to write it down.

8

"You don't have to continue this pregnancy."

Walls of shame broken down

Meet Corliss . . .

As a young girl I was always insecure. I know that is why I made a lot of the choices I made in life. I first became pregnant at the age of 16. At that time I chose life for my child and married my high school sweetheart. But just before my 20th birthday, our marriage was in serious trouble and we did not think we were going to make it. We had an adorable 2-year-old son and a beautiful baby daughter that was only 2 months old, and my doctor told me I was expecting again. I had been suffering from postpartum depression and I broke down in tears when the doctor gave me the news. His first words to me were, **"You don't have to continue this pregnancy".** This was the same man that had delivered my beautiful children.

When I left the hospital that day, my life was changed forever. I had such emptiness and a pain that I could not share with anyone.

I trusted him and allowed him to make all the arrangements never allowing myself to think about what I was doing. I know now that God was with me that day, and just waiting for me to turn to Him and say, "help me." But I didn't and when I left the hospital that day, my life was changed forever. I had such emptiness and a pain that I could not share with anyone not even my husband who went through this with me. God never left me even after I had failed Him. So, I went running toward God with all my heart and by His grace our marriage survived. But there was always that hurt and pain in the middle of us. Every time I would get closer to God, Satan would remind me of what I had done and **I would slip away again in shame.**

8

One night a wonderful friend took me to a fundraising dinner for the Burleson Pregnancy Aid Center and when I heard the speaker, she could have been telling my story. **I always thought I was the only woman in the world that could have made this choice.** That night somehow I managed to hold it together until I got home. God had started breaking down every wall of hurt, pain, and shame that I had buried for so long and had allowed Satan to use to keep me from experiencing everything God had for me. You see I was a Christian at the time, but I had made choices without going to God for help.

That night when I got home, I got down on my face in front of God and finally asked Jesus to help me, to take away my shame, my pain, and my sorrow. Jesus helped me find healing through a post-abortion bible study. And through His Word allowed me to give it all to him and in exchange gave me hope and joy again.

As I went through the recovery group bible study, Jesus also started working in my husband's life and gave us the marriage He always had planned for us. I now serve God by leading post-abortion recovery groups and counseling young women facing crisis pregnancies to help them make a different choice, to give them an opportunity to experience how wonderful it is to have an intimate relationship with Jesus Christ.

God has given me the confidence to know that through Him I can now help others to find that same healing and restoration with our Savior that I have found. I will never forget about that choice in life, but am so thankful that God is allowing me the opportunity to take the very worst event in my life and to use it to help others find Him and know how amazing His grace is. You see, He paid the price for my choice and for me.

– Corliss
Married with two children and five grandchildren
Director of Client Services

#2. POSITIVE THOUGHTS, WORDS, AND ACTIONS

We live in a universe that is governed by certain laws, which were put into motion by God Himself. One of those laws is called the law of sowing and reaping. The secular world refers to this law as the law of cause and effect. The law of cause and effect states that there are specific causes for success and likewise there are specific causes for failure. It's really not that difficult to understand.

One definition of insanity is to believe that you can keep doing what you've been doing and get different results.
– John Maxwell

If you are enjoying success in any area of your life, then you simply need to trace it back to what you did to have that success and then continue to repeat it. If you are experiencing failure, then trace it back to the cause and then stop doing it.

If you don't want to be a failure, then you have to learn certain laws that produce success. Once again, one of these laws is the law of seedtime and harvest or the law of cause and effect.

While the earth remaineth, seedtime and harvest, . . . shall not cease.
Genesis 8:22

The way you live today is the result of the seeds you've sown in the past. If you don't like the way you live, then you have no one to blame but yourself. You planted this garden. You sowed these seeds and now you are reaping them.

I want to encourage you to take the time to sit down and carefully look at what you have been doing that is preventing you from having success. Most importantly, let's look at what you've been saying out of your own mouth **about yourself.**

Whether you realize it or not, you're applying the law of cause and effect or as the Bible calls it, the law of sowing and reaping **every time you speak.** You are reaping today what you have spoken over yourself in the past.

Be not deceived; God is not mocked: for whatsoever a man soweth, that shall he also reap.

Galatians 6:7

A man's harvest in life depends entirely upon the seeds which he sows.

Galatians 6:7 (The Philips Translation)

The primary way that this is done is through thoughts, words, and actions. Your thoughts are seeds. Your words are seeds. And your actions are seeds.

If you don't like the harvest, stop planting it!

Many years ago, my friend Charles Capps asked me to come to England, Arkansas, to preach. We would fly in and land at his airport that was actually a strip cut right out in the middle of his cotton field.

Every time we would land our airplane at Charles' place, I would notice cotton on both sides of the landing strip. You could see cotton growing all over the place. On this occasion as we landed, I noticed that there wasn't any cotton growing. There was something growing, but I was not familiar with it. I didn't know what it was.

When we got to the end of the runway, Charles was standing there waiting for me. We cut the engines off, got out of the airplane, and Charles said, "Welcome to England, Arkansas. I'm glad you're here. Peggy has supper waiting for us. Let's go to the house."

I said, "Charles, where is your cotton?"

He said, "I didn't plant any. Do you have any luggage?"

I said, "You didn't plant any?"

He said, "You have any luggage?"

I said, "Well, why didn't you plant any?"

He said, "I didn't want any. Where is your luggage?"

I said, "Well, Charles, what is that growing out there?"

He said, "Soybeans."

I asked, "Why did you plant soybeans?"

He said, "I wanted it. Do you have anymore luggage?"

I thought to myself, *Now wait a minute. He used to have cotton. For years, he had cotton. Now he doesn't have cotton. Now he has soybeans. He didn't want cotton. He wanted soybeans. Is that the way this works?*

If you don't want cotton, then don't plant cotton. If you want soybeans, then plant soybeans. I got a wonderful revelation from talking to Charles. If you want change in your life then change what you've been planting.

Are you fed up with sickness and disease? Then stop sowing the seeds. *Oh you mean it is my fault I am sick?* It's very possible.

"I don't know why I always get the flu. If anybody's going to get the flu on our street, it will be me!" Those are seeds.

Quit sowing seeds of poverty and lack. *"I never have enough money. We never have enough! My daddy never had enough money. He was poor. I will probably be poor."* Those are seeds. If you don't like that crop, then quit planting the seeds. *"I hate the way I look. I'm so fat."* Stop sowing those seeds.

Death and life are in the power of the tongue: and they that love it shall eat the fruit thereof.

Proverbs 18:21

Prior to 1969, I didn't know that law was at work in my life. The only problem was, it was working against me instead of for me. But when I began to hear Kenneth Copeland, Oral Roberts, and Kenneth Hagin, I discovered I could change the harvest in my life by planting different seeds. Now I plant seeds of health. I plant seeds of prosperity. I don't talk lack and want. I talk good about myself and my future.

Where do you plant the seeds?

If you want to grow tomatoes where do you go to get those seeds? You go to the seed store. Is that correct? However, did you notice when you walked in the seed store that they aren't growing in the store? You don't have to work your way through the corn, and the cabbage, or step over the peas and the lettuce to get to the seeds you want. Why is it not growing in the seed store? Simply because that is not the proper environment for it.

Your Bible is the seed store, however the seeds won't grow in your Bible. What is the proper environment? It is your heart. When you take the seed of God's Word out of the seed store, and plant them in your heart, speak them **out of your mouth,** then eventually you will have the harvest that God promised you. It is a matter of understanding the basic spiritual laws. The law of sowing and reaping or the law of cause and effect is about as basic as you can get.

Change your thoughts and you change your world. – Norman Vincent Peale

If you don't like the harvest or the crop that is coming up in your life, then you have to take full responsibility. If you want different results, then you must plant different seeds. The primary way this is done is first of all through thoughts, secondly, through words, and thirdly, through your actions. Your thoughts, your words, and your actions are all seeds.

You will never get on the road to success as long as you continue to blame somebody else for your failure. You have got to take full responsibility for your own actions. Most people tend to blame others for their failures. To change failure into success demands that you take full responsibility for your own actions and then look closely at the seeds you've sown.

You have to take the time to just sit down and carefully look at what you have been doing and face the fact that you may be doing some things wrong.

God is the author of success. If you want to be successful, then go to His Word and discover the laws that He has set forth. If you properly appropriate those laws, then success will eventually come. Now if you are hoping for success overnight, then you are going to be disappointed. That is just not the way it works. Success is progressive.

Satan does not want you to succeed. He is against you and he hopes that you will never learn these laws. He hopes that you will give up.

Once again, everything that has happened in your life began with a thought and then was released through words and actions. If your thoughts were good or positive, then your words and your actions were positive and consequently, you got positive results.

On the other hand, if your thoughts were negative then your words and your actions were negative and consequently, you got negative results.

This is an immutable law which just simply means it's unchangeable. By accepting it as unchangeable then you will take control of your own destiny. Everything that you are or ever will be is a result of the way you think, talk, and act.

If you change the way you think, talk, and act and align them with the Word of God, then you will change the quality of your life.

If everything that is happening in your life seems to be negative or you are always in a crisis, then you need to take inventory of what you are *thinking*, what you are saying, and how you are *acting*. You can't change God's law, so you'll have to be the one who changes.

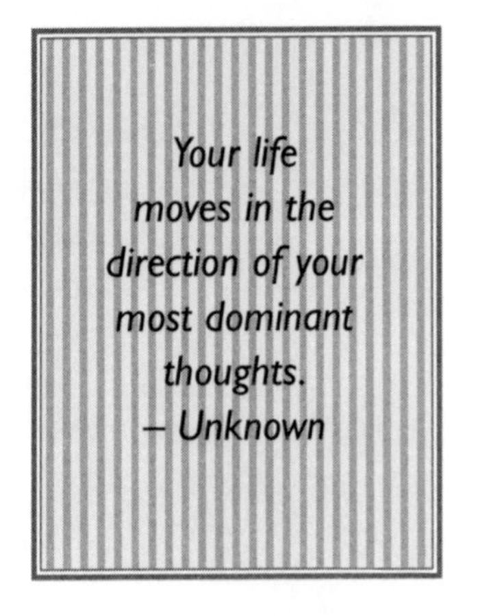

Be not deceived; God is not mocked: for whatsoever a man soweth, that shall he also reap.

Galatians 6:7

Back in 1969, I quit blaming others for my failures and my problems. I took full responsibility and began to renew my mind to the Word of God and found out that I can think, talk, and act differently.

You don't have to think like the rest of the world. You can talk differently. You can act differently. Sometimes you may feel like you are the only person in your neighborhood who believes this, but just keep living it and watch how the quality of your life, your self-image, your confidence, and your outlook on life will drastically change. Just remember that everything that you are and everything that you will ever be is the result of the way you think, talk, and act.

Cast down wrong thoughts

God's Word says, *bring every thought into captivity.* That just simply means to make every thought line up with the Word of God. If it does not line up with the Word of God, then cast it out. Don't think it anymore. Why? Because thoughts are seeds. That is how it all begins.

If you fail to cast those thoughts out of your mind, then they will eventually drop down into your heart. The Bible says, out of the abundance of your heart, your mouth will speak. If your thoughts are negative, then you are headed for a negative harvest. If they are positive, then you are headed for a positive harvest.

Refusing to think negative thoughts is not easy. Even after you read this book Satan will try to get you to think that it won't work for you. You have to **on purpose** cast those thoughts down. *How? Is that possible?* Yes. You can replace negative thoughts with positive thoughts. Start thinking what the Bible says. Instead of thoughts of lack, start thinking My God supplies all my need according to His riches in glory by Christ Jesus.

If you constantly think that you are not going to make it, and that you are going to lose everything you've got; then those dominant thoughts are going to take you in that direction. You are today and you will be tomorrow what you think about the most.

For as he thinketh in his heart, so is he . . .

Proverbs 23:7

So what are your most dominant thoughts? Do you think you're a failure or do you think that with God on your side, you can't help but succeed? Everything you are or ever will be is a result of the way you think. Wrong thinking can build a stronghold in your mind, which will limit you and rob you of God's best.

It is time to tear down the strongholds created by wrong thinking. Wrong thoughts create strongholds or barriers and it is only by thinking God's thoughts that these barriers will be destroyed.

Summing it all up, friends, I'd say you'll do best by filling your minds and meditating on things that are true, noble, reputable, authentic, compelling, gra-

cious – the best, not the worst; the beautiful; not the ugly; things to praise, not things to curse.

Philippians 4:8 (The Message Translation)

In other words, be selective about what you think. When you think on what God thinks, then it will produce a very positive outlook in your life. It will create expectation. Not only that, it will create enthusiasm.

Thinking the way God thinks puts you in control of what happens to you. It puts you in control of your destiny. The quicker you begin to reject thoughts that exalt themselves against the knowledge of God, then the sooner you will move into what God says is yours! In the eyes of God, you are a winner. Think of yourself the way God sees you. He sees you as a champion in Christ.

Finally, brethren, whatsoever things are true, whatsoever things are honest, whatsoever things are just, whatsoever things are pure, whatsoever things are lovely, whatsoever things are of good report; . . . think on these things.

Philippians 4:8

Once again, success is simply understanding basic spiritual laws. When you learn how to properly appropriate these laws, then they are going to work for you instead of against you.

It is never too late to start applying God's Word in your life. If these concepts are all new to you, then start applying them today. Make the decision that you are going to live this way for the rest of your life. It won't all happen overnight, but it will happen. If you could see where my wife Carolyn and I were thirty-six years ago when we first began to learn these laws and where we are today, then you would certainly have to agree that it works. And if it can work for Jerry and Carolyn, then it can and will work for you.

9

"Dear God, help me to not be silly."

From "different" to making a difference

Meet "Fluffy" the Clown . . .

When I was a little girl, I had many friends and loved school. I loved the books and stories and some of my favorite things to do were coloring and painting. The only problem was, I realized that I was so silly and everyone laughed at the things I said. I tried very hard not to be silly but I just couldn't seem to help myself. At the end of the day, I would tell myself, "Tomorrow I will not be silly. I will be different." When the next day would come, I was still silly. So I started praying to God to help me not to be silly. At the end of the school year, I would think, "Ok, next year I will be different." I prayed all summer, "Dear God, help me to not be silly. Help me to be different when I go back to school the next year. I'll have a lot of new friends and they won't know the 'silly' me and I can start over." Well, I went back to school and I was still the same.

I grew up and married and had a family. I was still silly. Then one day I met a new friend who was a clown and another one who was going to clown school to learn how to be a clown. So I went also. I learned how to put on make-up and dress like a clown but I didn't feel like a clown. Then I started going to the children's hospital and the nursing homes and other places. The little children laughed and were so happy to see me and so were the older people. I could make them smile and laugh with my silliness. They made me laugh and smile and have a nice warm feeling inside.

9

I started to realize that being silly was not something to be ashamed of but actually a gift from God. He didn't take away my silliness. He knew that it could be used for Him. He wanted me to be the way I am, not different. He loves me. You know God gives us our gifts. Not everyone has the same one. He knows what we can do. He knows every hair on our head and every freckle we have. He knew us before we were born. He wants us to recognize what our gift is and use it for His glory. That silly little girl is called "Fluffy" the clown.

A joyful heart is good medicine . . .
Proverbs 17:22 (New American Standard)

– "Fluffy"
Widowed with two children and four grandchildren
Clown
62

#3. PERCEPTION

In order to be totally free to be yourself and stay that way, you have to learn how to become perceptive. What do I mean by that? You must learn to see every situation **from God's viewpoint.**

While we look not at things which are seen, but at the things which are not seen: for the things which are seen are temporal . . .

II Corinthians 4:18

Do you know what ***temporal*** means? Years ago the Holy Spirit gave me this definition: *subject to change.*

Paul is telling us that if you can **see it,** then it is subject to change. It is not permanent. A financial crisis is not permanent. It is subject to change. Sickness and disease are not permanent, they are subject to change. Jesus proved that every day in his ministry. He proved that leprosy was subject to change. He even proved that blindness was subject to change. He proved that dead folks were subject to change. So in order to stay free, you must become perceptive, that is, be able to see every situation from God's viewpoint.

If you could see what I see . . .

I once heard a story about a little boy who found out that the circus was coming to his hometown. He could hardly wait. His mother told him that there was going to be a parade and that it would be coming right in front of their house.

This little boy got so excited that he could hardly sleep. So the next morning as the parade began, he got out in his front yard. His mother said, "Son, you can't get out of the yard because there is going to be a lot of traffic and a lot of people in the street and I don't want you to get hurt so you have to watch the parade from the front yard."

Well, they had a fence around their yard. So the only way that he could see the parade was by looking through the cracks in the board fence. He couldn't see very much. He could only see what was right in front of him. However, he had an older brother who was upstairs. The older brother was looking out of his window. He could not only see what had already gone by, but, he could see what was happening right in front of him, and he could also see what was coming. Why? Because of his vantage point. He was up high where he could see the whole thing.

He kept shouting down to his little brother. "Come on up here." The little brother kept saying, "No, I will miss the parade." All he could see was what was right in front of him. Little did he know that if he had gone upstairs, he would have seen the whole thing – past, present, and future.

Do you understand what I am saying? That is the way most Christians live, looking through the fence. All they see is what is right in front of them, and you can tell that by the way they talk because all they talk about is the problem. They are problem-oriented rather than solution-oriented.

Every problem has a solution

People who fail usually do so because of wrong perception. It is unlikely that they will be free until they first become perceptive or in other words, be able to look beyond the problem and see the solution. Every problem has a solution. Every test is a potential testimony.

We are troubled on every side, yet not distressed; we are perplexed, but not in despair; Persecuted, but not forsaken; cast down, but not destroyed.

II Corinthians 4:8-9

Notice all the *buts* and the *yets* in those verses. If you don't read the buts and the yets, it turns out this way – **We are troubled on every side. We are perplexed, persecuted, and cast down.** That is the way religion reads it, but it is not the way Paul wrote it.

He said, we are **troubled on every side *yet* not distressed. We are perplexed *but* not in despair. Persecuted *but* not forsaken. Cast down *but* not destroyed.**

One translation says – *You might knock me down, but you will never knock me out.* That is a winner's attitude.

Now thanks be unto God, which always causeth us to triumph in Christ . . .

II Corinthians 2:14

I am glad Paul put ***always*** in that verse. That means that you can be a winner every time. Actually God expects you to be.

Triumph is always God's best for our lives. No matter how difficult or how impossible the situation might look, *triumph always* is God's will. So therefore, if you know that God said that and God is not a man that He should lie; then you can be persistent because you have perceived that God's best in this situation is for you to triumph. If God is on your side and no weapon formed against you prospers, then you can stand against anything that Satan throws your way.

Perception changes everything

By changing how you perceive your problems, you can literally change your life from failure and defeat to victory and success.

A very simple illustration is David and Goliath. When David saw Goliath, his perception of that challenge was totally different from that of his brothers and the entire armies of Israel. When the armies of Israel saw Goliath, they perceived that he was too big to kill. When David looked at him, he thought he was too big to miss. Same giant, same problem, a different perception.

You are created by God to succeed and not fail. Success does not come without adversity. There is no such thing as success without adversity. Well-known entrepreneur, J. C. Penny, was asked one time the secret to his success and he just simply said, "adversity." He said, "I would never have amounted to anything had I not been forced to come up the hard way."

Most people run from adversity. They don't want adversity and yet this man was saying that he thrived on it. It is what got him where he was. He learned how to have a different perception than that of others.

A winner all along

For I know that this shall turn to my salvation . . .

Philippians 1:19

Paul was *in prison* when he wrote this, but he remained positive. He expected every situation to turn for his good. He also said in that same verse,

For I know that this shall turn to my salvation through your prayer, and the supply of the Spirit of Jesus Christ.

Philippians 1:19

He knew that prayer changes things and he knew that the Holy Spirit had a supply that would cause every situation to turn for his good.

If you enjoy football, then you might remember a man named Tom Dempsey. Tom Dempsey was born with a handicap. One of his legs had half a foot. He loved football but people told him that he couldn't play football because of his handicap. But all of his life, his mother and father told him, "Tom, you can do anything you believe you can do."

He would not accept what everybody else said. Eventually he was drafted by the San Diego Chargers but later he was cut from the team and the New Orleans Saints took him. They needed a field goal kicker and that was his specialty. But unlike most field goal kickers he kicked the football with half a foot!

In one particular game where the Saints needed a field goal to win in the closing seconds of the ball game, the coach put Tom Dempsey on the field and Tom kicked a record-breaking field goal with half a foot! He kicked the ball sixty-three yards!

How did he do that? Because he would not accept a loser's mentality even though he was handicapped. The sports world went wild. It was the longest field goal ever kicked in professional football history and he was the hero!

People couldn't believe it. The media said he was a record-breaker, a history-maker, and the greatest field goal kicker ever. They asked him, "How does it feel?" "How did you do it?" He said, "My mother and father told me from day one that I could do anything I believed I could do." He said, "I have been a winner all my life. You folks are just now finding it out."

Isn't that great? Do you know what that tells me? Down on the inside of you, there is a winner. There is a champion down there. The world may not know it yet. Your family may not know it yet. Your friends may not know it yet, but down on the inside of you, there is a winner. That winner wants to come out. This is your time.

Is it just your imagination?

All things are possible to those who believe. Don't be so quick to accept defeat. God is on your side. And that means that failure is never inevitable. No matter what you go through, no matter how impossible it looks, no matter how severe the pressure may be, you have the God-given ability on the inside of you to rise above it. Train yourself to always think, "How does God see this situation?"

A beautiful illustration of it is in the story of Caleb. He was one of the men sent out by Moses to spy the land. God had told them that the land was theirs. He said that it flowed with milk and honey and it belonged to them. All the spies came back and reported to the congregation that the land was exactly the way God said it was. It flowed with milk and honey. But then ten of those spies made this comment – "but we are not able to take the land." They said, "There are giants in the land and we are but grasshoppers in their sight" (Author's paraphrase). Now that was a lie because not one of those spies walked up to one of the giants and asked, "Would you please tell us how you perceive us?" No. It was just their imagination.

The greatest battle you will ever fight in your life is between your ears – in your mind. They didn't know what those people were thinking. They just assumed they thought of them as grasshoppers. Caleb was the first to speak up and he said, "We are well able. Give us this place. Let's go up at once. It is just as God said and we are well able to take the land" (Author's paraphrase).

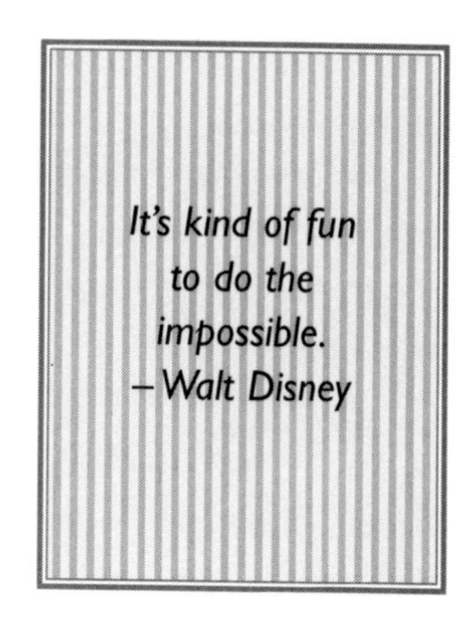

Notice he saw the same giants they saw, but his outlook was totally different. They saw giants who considered them grasshoppers. Caleb saw giants who could be defeated. Same giants, same problem, different perception.

God said that Caleb had a different spirit. What is a different spirit? Someone who has the ability to see as God sees. Someone who perceives as God perceives and is willing to stand against adversity no matter how long it takes to win.

Learn to look at every situation, every problem, and every challenge from God's viewpoint realizing that they are subject to change. When you know that your problems are subject to change, then you can endure anything that the devil puts in your path.

#4. PERSISTENCE

When going after the dreams, goals, and purpose for your life, another principle that you must always apply is persistence. To give up is to invite defeat. To keep on giving up is to create a defeat mentality.

If you keep giving up then it won't take near as much pressure the next time for you to give up because you have created a habit in your life. Sometimes habits are hard to break, but they can be broken, however it will take the Word of God to do it.

Jesus Himself said *if you continue in My Word, you will be my disciple indeed.* (A disciple is a disciplined one) *and you will know the truth and the truth will make you free.*

John 8:31-32

The act of continuing creates a habit. Anything you continue to do is going to become habitual to you. Well, you can create the habit of winning. You can create the habit of being persistent. You can create the habit of setting goals, and achieving each and every one of them.

Don't quit

This book has been written to help you to be free to be yourself, and to be the person God made you to be. Obviously Satan will not just roll over, play dead, and let you accomplish this without a fight.

He doesn't want your life story or your life's experiences to encourage anyone else. Why? Because it proves he's defeated and it proves that the Blood of Jesus worked.

So how can he stop you? By getting you to doubt yourself, your calling, your uniqueness, your forgiveness, and ultimately try to get you to just give up!

I have always been a Green Bay Packers' fan. When I was a kid, I used to watch the Green Bay Packers and of course Vince Lombardi was the head coach at that time. Back then, they were a dynasty. They were professional football. Vince Lombardi was a great motivator and a great leader. Someone asked him one time how he felt about his team losing a championship game one year. He said, "We didn't lose. We just ran out of time."

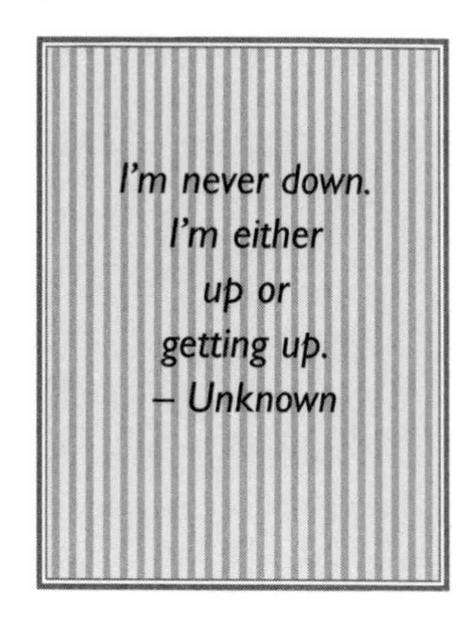

Winning was very important to him, and that is what he instilled into his players. Many of the men who had played for him said, "He not only taught us how to win in football, but he also taught us how to be winners off the field."

Determine in your own heart that you will become the winner that God has called you to be. When you determine that quitting is no longer an option in your life, then you are going to develop a winning lifestyle. You may have setbacks but those setbacks are temporary. They are not permanent. Every successful person has had setbacks, but the difference between them and others is that successful people do not quit.

You are not a loser. You are a winner. Learn to be persistent. You are not going to stay free to be yourself and accomplish all God has for you if you are going to quit every time there is pressure. You have what it takes to win. Keep telling yourself that. Stick with it and refuse to give up. It's well worth it. Trust me.

Persistence is always rewarded.

God honors those who honor His Word.
God honors those who are obedient to His commands.
God honors those who establish an unwavering stand against adversity.
God honors those who are willing to face persecution from others because of their uncompromising stand.
God honors those who constantly demonstrate an unwavering commitment to never give up.
God honors those who persistently pursue His promises.

Persistence is a key to being all God made you to be.

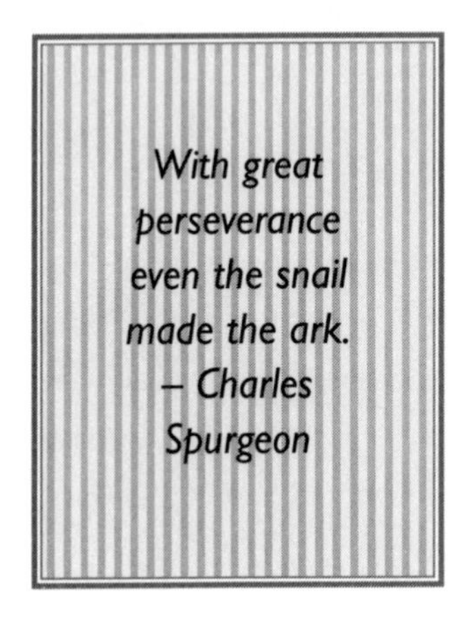

Don't settle for average

The reason why so many Christians do not win is because it takes discipline to be a winner. Most people don't like that word. However if you're going to be a winner then you are going to ***have*** to discipline yourself. You'll have to make some rules for yourself that perhaps the average Christian would not make.

Do you not know in a race all the runners compete, but [only] one receives the prize? So run [your race] that you may lay hold [of the prize] and make it yours. Now every athlete that goes into training conducts himself temperately and restricts himself in all things. They do it to win a wreath that will soon wither . . .

I Corinthians 9:24-25 (Amplified)

I remember back in 1984, Carolyn and I went with some friends to the Olympics in Los Angeles. We went to all of the boxing matches we could get into. We saw Evander Holyfield compete. I told Carolyn, "That man will one day be heavyweight champion of the world." And even though a lot of people didn't think so, he did become the heavyweight champion four times.

You don't get where Mr. Holyfield got without discipline. You don't get where he got without persistence. I guarantee you that there are things he put himself through that most people would not even consider doing. Why? Because he wanted to win. He wanted to be a winner. A lot of Christians see other Christians winning and they wish they could have what they have, but they will not do what is necessary to win. It's only when you get desperate to win that you will finally be willing to do whatever it takes.

Discipline – this is what makes a winner out of you.

You've been to the stadium and seen the athletes race. Everyone runs; one wins. Run to win. All good athletes train hard. They do it for a gold medal that tarnishes and fades. You're after one that's gold eternally. I don't know about you, but I'm running hard for the finish line. I'm giving it everything I've got. No sloppy living for me! I'm staying alert and in top condition. I'm not going to get caught napping, telling everyone else all about it and then missing out myself.

I Corinthians 9:24-27 (The Message Translation)

Don't just get in the race but run to win. Go for the above and beyond. Don't be satisfied with being average. Determine that you will excel in everything you do.

Don't accept failure

A man came to Thomas Edison one time after he had experimented 1,000 times trying to develop the light bulb, and said, "Mr. Edison, you have failed 1,000 times." Thomas Edison said, "I did not fail 1,000 times. I have discovered 1,000 ways it will not work. I am 1,000 ways closer to finding the way it will work." He wouldn't accept failure.

Don't accept defeat

Years ago, I was invited to preach in Dr. Lester Sumrall's church and his son, Peter, picked me up at the airport. Peter said, "Brother Jerry, did you hear that our television station burned down?"

I said, "No, I didn't. When did this happen?"

He said, "Just a few days ago."

I said, "Well, what did your father say?" Peter said, "Dad was out of town preaching when it happened. We all thought, *how are we going to tell daddy.* So when he arrived, we all went to the airport to meet him and when we got him in the car, we finally got the courage to tell him." We said, "Daddy, the television station burned down while you were gone. Do you want to go see it?"

> ***Success is not final, failure is not fatal: it is the courage to continue that counts.***
> ***– Winston Churchill***

Brother Sumrall said, "Why would I want to look at ashes? Build it back!"

He would not accept defeat. Too many times we want the results of a Thomas Edison or a Lester Sumrall or anybody else that we believe is a great achiever, but they did not get that way by quitting every time there was opposition. They got that way by persevering.

No turning back

Give ear, O my people, to my law: incline your ears to the words of my mouth. I will open my mouth in a parable. I will utter dark sayings of old: Which we have heard and known, and our fathers have told us. We will not hide them from their children, showing to the generation to come the praises of the Lord, and his strength, and his wonderful works which he hath done.

For he established a testimony in Jacob, and appointed a law in Israel, which he commanded our fathers, that they should make them known to their children: That the generation to come might know them, even the children which should be born; who should arise and declare them to their children: That they might set their hope in God, and not forget the works of God, but keep his commandments: And might not be as their fathers, a stubborn and rebellious generation; a generation that set not their heart aright and whose spirit was not ***steadfast*** *with God.*

Psalm 78:1-8

The Spirit of God said these words to me one time while I was reading those verses, "Every failure in the body of Christ is due to a lack of steadfastness." Notice it says – *Don't be like these people who did not set their hearts aright whose spirit was not steadfast with God.* And then the Bible gives an example of the children of Ephraim.

. . . being armed, and carrying bows, turned back in the day of battle.

Psalm 78:9

Even though they were equipped, even though they were qualified, and skillful, they accepted defeat and they turned back in the day of battle.

Too many times we are too quick to give in and to give up. Persistence is what it takes to be victorious in every adversity. Determine today that "turning back" is no longer an option in your life.

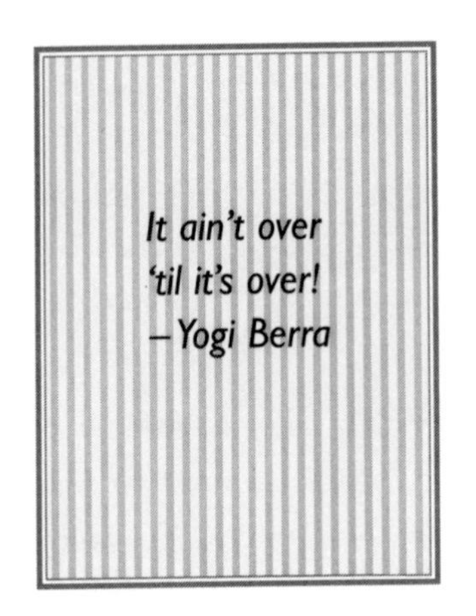

Kenneth Hagin used to say that if you will prepare to stand forever, then it will not take very long. Make up your mind that regardless of how long it takes, you are not going to give in.

#5. PASSION

The theme of our Bible correspondence school is a passion for God, a passion for souls, and a passion for life. If you're passionate about something, you won't let anything stand between you and it. Desire and passion are the greatest motivators for getting results. The greatest obstacle to your success and the tactic Satan uses the most to destroy your passion is the fear of failure.

The fear of failure

The words that are the greatest enemy to your faith are found in Genesis 3:10. This is after Adam had committed high treason against God. Sin had been committed. God had created Adam in His likeness. God expected him to live by faith. After the fall, and after sin had been committed, we find these words when God asked Adam where he was.

. . . I heard thy voice in the garden, and I was afraid, because I was naked; and I hid myself.

Genesis 3:10

Notice these three words – *I was afraid.* Those three words are the greatest enemy to your faith. Fear is the opposite of faith and fear will rob you of God's best. God did not give you the spirit of fear.

For God hath not given us the spirit of fear; but of power, and of love, and of a sound mind.

II Timothy 1:7

For God did not give us a spirit of timidity (of cowardice, of craven and cringing and fawning fear), but [He has given us a spirit] of power and of love and of calm and well-balanced mind and discipline and self-control.

II Timothy 1:7 (Amplified)

It is fear that causes you to settle for far less than what God has in mind for your life. The fear of failure is probably the greatest single obstacle a believer has to overcome. Everyone has experienced failure in some way or another. Many people never recover from the experience of it. If you have ever failed at anything, then Satan would love to use that as an obstacle or a barrier in your life so that you never have confidence to step out again.

No inhibitions

Let me tell you something about fear. You weren't born with it. It is something that you learned. Psychologists tell us that babies are born with two remarkable qualities. Number one, they are born largely unafraid. A baby does not come into this world with a fear of failure.

The other quality that a child is born with is no inhibitions. They have no fear of failure and no inhibitions. Babies just do whatever they want to do, at any place and at any time. Did you notice that an infant does not ask its parents if it is okay to cry in a public place? They don't care. They think every place is the right place for them to cry just as loud as they desire.

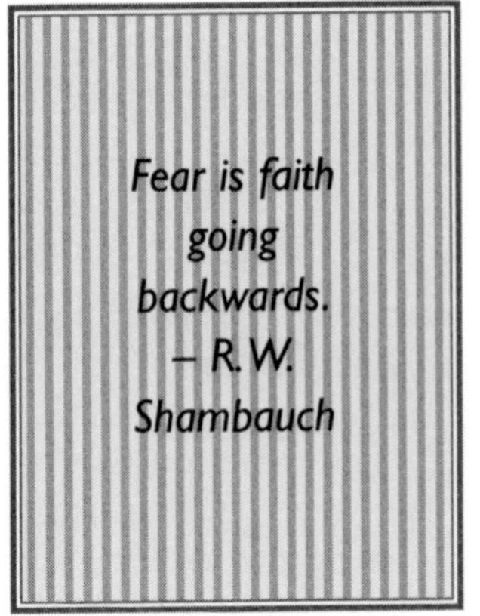

You came into this earth without fear and without inhibitions. If you have fear in your life and you are inhibited then you had to learn that. You had to develop that. It did not come at birth and God did not give you a spirit of fear. We even say things like, "I have *developed* a fear of flying." You weren't born with that, you developed it!

Fear is a spiritual force and it is what activates Satan just like faith activates God. Fear attracts Satan in your life just as faith attracts God. Fear invites Satan to manifest himself just like faith invites God to manifest himself.

Fear is nothing more than confidence in the devil. It is the reciprocal of faith. Just like hate is the reciprocal of love. God is ready to take you higher in your life but you first have to conquer the fear of failure.

Master your fears

If you let fear control you, then you will

not reach your full potential and you will never be free to be yourself.

God expects you to be fearless and bold in the face of all adversity. If you are going to experience God's best, then it is mandatory that you conquer fear and especially the fear of failure. The fear of failure robs you of thinking big and expecting big things in your life. The fear of failure will keep you from stepping out and doing something new or something different.

Fear can immobilize you. If you are immobilized by fear, then you will settle for less than God's best. Just as confidence is the result of meditating God's Word, fear is the result of meditating on what the devil says. If you think about what the devil says long enough, it will create fear. Fear brings him on the scene just like faith brings God on the scene.

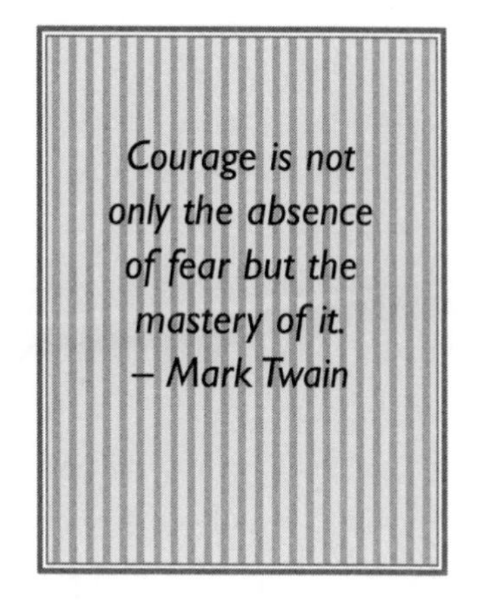

People of courage are not people who have never had fear. People who have courage are people who have mastered fear.

When I was growing up, one of my heroes was Audi Murphy. He became a movie star who played in a lot of Westerns but before that he was a World War II veteran who was one of the most highly decorated men in the history of military service. I guess one of the reasons I was so attracted to him was because he was short like me. I saw his life story in the movie called *To Hell and Back* and then I also read the biography about his life.

He was absolutely amazing during World War II. I mean he, single-handedly, took out entire German companies. It wasn't that he didn't have fear he just learned how to master it. Often, there would be bodies piled up all around him and the rest of his buddies in the service would just stand around and shake their heads. They could not believe what this man would do.

When nothing's going good for you

II Kings 7 is one of my favorite stories in the Bible. It speaks of a time when the people of God had been completely surrounded by enemy forces to the point they had completely cut off their supply lines. There was no food. Everybody was starving. The prophet said by utterance of the Holy Ghost (and I am paraphrasing) that God was going to turn things around. Well, it was hard for anybody to believe that because the situation was so devastating. The enemy was either going to starve them to death or they would invade and kill them all. So it looked as though it was a hopeless situation. But the prophet said that things were going to change and that God was going to turn everything around.

Outside the camp were four lepers. These lepers were in a more critical situation than the people inside the camp. They had three strikes against them. Number one – There was nothing to eat so they could die of starvation. Number two – The enemy was coming so they could die by the sword. Number three – Leprosy could kill them. They had nothing going for them.

It looked like the only thing to do was just sit there until they died. That is what a lot of Christians do. Rather than conquer their fear, they just sit there and let the devil take over and rob them of what rightfully belongs to them. Finally, in verse three, it says, *and they said one to another why sit we here until we die?*

I love that. I have preached some of the most powerful sermons that I have ever preached on those seven words. *Why sit we here until we die.* In other words, if we are going to die, then let's die in action rather than just sit here and accept defeat. If we are going to die, then we are going to die doing something.

Those lepers would not accept defeat even though they didn't have anything going for them. At least the people in the camp had all their flesh intact. They were starving and the enemy was about to invade, but they were not nearly as bad off as those lepers. But notice who got the job done. It was four helpless, hopeless, impossible-looking lepers, who decided they were not going to let fear control their lives anymore. They got up and started moving toward the enemy's camp. When they did, God got right in the middle of what they were doing, amplified their footsteps, and made it sound like an entire army coming over the hill and it absolutely frightened the enemy to the point that they ran away and left all the food, all the gold, and all the silver. Four lepers came over the hill and there was not a soul to fight! They marched into the enemy's camp and took back everything that was stolen.

The more you fear something, the more likely you are to attract it.
– Jerry Savelle

God is looking for some courageous people like these four lepers today. God is looking for some people who will master their fears.

Why sit we here until we die? That ought to be your theme. Courage comes every time you look fear right in the face and decide you are going forward.

Now faith is the substance of things hoped for . . .

Hebrews 11:1

If faith is the substance of things hoped for, then fear gives substance to the things you dread. So if you keep confessing your fear, then what you fear will eventually manifest in your life. Fear is like a magnet. Job once said that the thing he so greatly feared eventually materialized.

For the thing which I greatly feared has come upon me, and that which I was afraid of is come unto me.

Job 3:25

You will never find a person who has great faith and great fear at the same time. One negates the other. When faith comes, fear goes; but if you are not in the Word of God, then fear comes and faith goes. You are attracting one or the other into your life every day based upon what you listen to and what you see.

Your eyes and your ears are the gateway to your spirit. What you see and what you hear will get down into your spirit. We know that, by and large, we live in a world that is full of negative information. It is against our faith. It is against the knowledge of God. From time to time, we all have the opportunity to be in a negative atmosphere and to hear negative things. If you have a television set, then you have an opportunity to hear negative things every day. If you work in an environment where most of the people are not born-again, then you probably hear negative things every day.

Doubts are nothing more than faith in what the devil says and that it will come to pass. If you doubt God, then that means you have confidence in what the devil says. Jesse Duplantis says if you are going to doubt anything, then *doubt your doubts.*

If you fail to conquer the fears that you have allowed to come into your life, then you are never going to be free to be yourself and do what God put you on this earth to do. To master the fear of failure you must do these things:

#1. **Begin to see yourself as God sees you.** That's what this entire book is about. Meditate on who God says you are.

Start talking about yourself the way God sees you. God is looking through the Blood of Jesus. God sees you as more than a conqueror. He sees you as the redeemed of the Lord.

There is a direct relationship between how vividly you can see yourself as God sees you and how rapidly you become that person. In other words, the more faithful you are about spending time in God's Word, then the quicker you will become the person that God sees.

#2. **You must become passionate and enthusiastic about what God says you can do.** The word ***enthusiasm*** comes from a Greek word which literally means *God-inspired* and *God-in.* When you are enthusiastic, that means that you can see God in every situation. Others may not be able to see what you see, but you see victory and success coming your way. You can see God at work in your behalf and it creates enthusiasm.

Enthusiasm and passion deepens your faith. Nothing great is ever achieved without them. You must be enthusiastic about whatever you do. You have to be passionate about establishing a ministry, or building a church, or about starting a business. Once again, nothing great is ever achieved without it.

#3. **Constantly affirm to yourself who you are, what you are, and what you can do in Christ Jesus.** I realize this sounds so basic and you may have already heard it 9,000 times but you are not going to be free to be you nor will you be the success that you are destined to be until you act on them every day of your life.

What does it mean ***to affirm?*** Affirmations are strong statements regarding what you believe. Affirming who you are and what you can do changes what is on the outside to what you see on the inside. Keep your conversation throughout the day consistent with what you believe God is saying about you. Remember to guard your mouth!

#4. **Feed your spirit daily on God's Word and faith-building material.** The more you read, the more you listen, and the more you watch faith-building programs, the less you will have to deal with fear because faith will come and fear will go. Be very selective about what you read, what you watch, and what you listen to.

#5. **Associate with winners.** Associate with people who have conquered fear. Associate with winners. Stay away from people who constantly talk fear and stay away from people who constantly talk failure. Success breeds success and failure breeds failure. Who you associate with has everything to do with your outcome.

He that walketh with wise men shall be wise: but a companion of fools shall be destroyed.

Proverbs 13:20

#6. POWERFUL FINISH

Growing up with a dad who repaired wrecked cars and restored antique and classic automobiles, I can still remember the first car that he ever gave me. I was only thirteen years old. Country boys learned to drive at an early age. So when I was thirteen years old, my dad gave me a 1929 Model-A Ford Coupe. Oh, I wish I still had it.

It was beat up and had a lot of rust on it and so Dad was going to help me restore it. I was taking it apart one day like I had seen my daddy do. I was trying to take the front bumper off. That bumper had probably not been touched since 1929. I had my wrench on that old bolt and nut and I was trying to break it loose but it just wouldn't give.

All of a sudden, Dad's hand came on top of my hand. I didn't even know that he had come near. I was underneath the bumper just giving it all I could and all of a sudden, his hand, which was much bigger and stronger than mine, was on the top of my hand, and Dad broke it loose! Every time I think of God's grace, I picture my dad's hand. He did what I could not do on my own. That's what grace is. It's when God puts his hand on your hand and gets the job done.

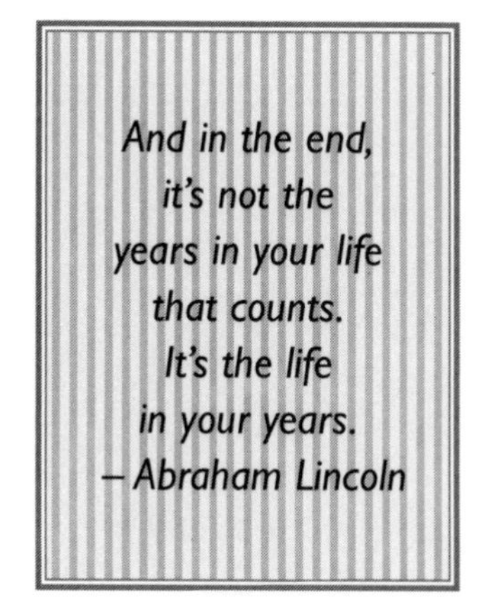

God's grace is sufficient. However if you give up, then where is God going to put his hand? If you quit under pressure, then you literally tie God's hands. He has nothing to work with. You have to give God something to work with.

. . . forgetting those things which are behind, and reaching forth unto those things which are before.

Philippians 3:13

In other words, forget the past. Even if you have made mistakes, even if you have failed, even if every goal you have set in the past never came close to being achieved, you have got to forget the past.

If you refuse to forget the past, then it is going to control your present and it is going to foul up your future. Let go of the past. Keep going forward!

Don't ever give up on your goals. Keep pursuing them with everything that is within you and always remember that God is your helper. When you feel like you can't do anymore, expect God's hand to come on your hand and help you get the job done.

> ***People often say that motivation doesn't last. Well, neither does bathing – that's why we recommend it daily.***
> ***– Zig Ziglar***

You owe it to yourself to find out what God wants you to accomplish and then refuse to back off. If it doesn't happen in a week, refuse to quit. If it doesn't happen in a month, don't quit. If it doesn't happen in a year, don't give up.

Make perseverance such a part of your lifestyle that you don't even have to think about it. Get to the place in your life that you never get up in the morning wondering if you should continue to stand, or should you give up. Get to the point where standing on the Word is such an ingrained characteristic that you don't even have to think about it. Your orders from heaven are to win; so don't give up until you do.

Be a winner. Don't settle for just the norm. Go all the way; don't just be a good starter. Determine to have a powerful finish! The only way that you will stay as you are is if you choose to do so. Destiny is not a matter of chance. Destiny is a matter of choice. Choose to have a bright future.

I call heaven and earth to record this day against you, that I have set before you life and death, blessings and cursing: therefore choose life . . .

Deuteronomy 30:19

You are experiencing right now in your life what you have chosen. If you are miserable, if you have low self-esteem, if you just feel like you are just here with no purpose in your life, then it is your choices that put you there.

But you don't have to stay there. Choose to have a good life. Don't let anybody determine how your life will turn out. One of the greatest things that God has ever done for human beings is to give us a will and the right to choose. You determine your destiny by making the right choices. God wants to help you make the right choices. That's why He has given you a blueprint and a plan in the Bible.

If you don't like the way you are presently living, then it's time to make some choices. If you don't like where you are, then you have got some decisions to make. And once you make them, don't let the devil talk you out of them. Determine to <u>continue</u> in what you've learned in this book and finish strong.

Finish with joy

But none of these things move me, neither count I my life dear unto myself, so that I might ***finish my course with joy*** *...*

Acts 20:24

To finish his course with joy was one of the goals that the Apostle Paul had set for himself. He was determined that nothing was going to stop him from accomplishing that goal. **"None of these things move me."** He is referring to opposition, adversity, challenges, tests, and trials. The Apostle Paul obviously had a lot of them. I call him the "apostle of confrontation."

A few verses earlier in verse 19 he makes this statement – *Serving the Lord with all humility of mind, and with* *many tears, and temptations* *...*

Have you ever shed tears as a result of your walk with God? We don't like to talk about the tears but sometimes they come. Sometimes things just don't happen as quickly as we thought they would. Sometimes we stand and we believe and we do everything we know to do and yet it looks like it is never going to come to pass. Sometimes it brings tears.

Paul also said he had many *temptations*. The literal Greek defines the word temptations as "testings and trials." So notice he said, *Serving the Lord with all humility of mind, and with many tears and temptations,...* and that is the reason he said **none of these things move me.**

That has become one of my favorite verses over the last thirty-six years. In fact, I have made it one of my mottos. None of these things move me.

Smith Wigglesworth used to say – **I am not moved by what I see. I am not moved by what I hear. I am not moved by what I feel. I am moved only by what I believe and I believe the Word of God.**

The goal of Paul was that he might finish his course with joy. Notice he didn't say, "My goal is that I might start the course." Now for a lot of people that would be a major accomplishment just to get started. But notice he's saying, *my goal is not only to start but to finish what I started* (Author's paraphrase). A lot of people start but they do not finish.

If you read Paul's life story, it becomes obvious that this man faced a lot of adversity; yet his goal was that he might ***finish his*** course with joy. He kept his eyes on the prize, so to speak. Because he was focused, God honored his unwavering stand; and I believe He will honor yours and mine as well.

I have fought a good fight, I have finished my course, I have kept the faith.
II Timothy 4:7

He said, "I have finished my course," which was the goal that he had established way back at the beginning of his walk with God. Was this easy for Paul? No, it was not. Once again, he had many tears, many temptations, many tests, many trials, and many adversities; and yet he stayed focused and he was able to persevere so that he could say at the end of his life, "I have finished my course."

In other words, he accomplished his mission. That is what God wants you to be able to say at the end of your life. You can do this if you'll just determine that giving up is no longer an option.

Laying aside every weight

Wherefore seeing we also are compassed about with so great a cloud of witnesses, let us lay aside every weight, and the sin which doth so easily beset us, and let us run with patience the race that is set before us,

Looking unto Jesus the author and finisher of our faith; who for the joy that was set before him endured the cross, despising the shame, and is set down at the right hand of the throne of God.

For consider him that endured such contradiction of sinners against himself, lest ye be wearied and faint in your minds.

Ye have not yet resisted unto blood, striving against sin.

Hebrews 12:1-4

If we are looking unto Jesus while we run the race that is set before us, then we will not have our eyes on all of the distractions that are around us. While we are running, we are to lay aside every weight and every sin. This is not a 100-yard dash. It is a lifetime race, a cross-country race, an endurance race. In such a race, we don't give it all we've got for just a short distance. We must pace ourselves for the long haul. That way, as we approach the end of our course, we will have something in reserve for a strong finish.

This is the way God expects His Church to finish; not beaten down, or worn out. Our Father wants us to finish with a strong "kick" for His glory.

Look unto Jesus every day, and run to win the race that is set before you. As you run, weights can become attached to you. So you have to determine that you will keep yourself free of anything that will interfere with your progress.

As you run the race of life, you must cleanse yourself of any accumulated weight such as sin. Unless you deal with the sin in your life, you will become so burdened down, that you can hardly run anymore.

Hebrews 12:1 tells us to **lay aside every weight.** How do we do that? How do you lay something aside? A weight is an inanimate object. It has no life or movement of its own. Unless it is moved by an outside force, it will remain wherever it is placed.

If I removed my coat and laid it aside, unless moved by someone else, that coat would stay where it was placed until I took it back up and put it back on. It has no ability to get back on me by itself. I must take it back upon myself.

So it is with sin. Sin cannot remain in your life unless you allow it to do so. It cannot get back on you unless you reach for it, receive it, or entertain it. If you lay that sin aside and refuse to receive it back, then it cannot abide in you any longer.

God doesn't want us to be victims of sin. He wants us to deal with it, get rid of it, and lay it aside. Daily communion with God should be the aim of every believer. The result will be growing in holiness and becoming closer to fulfilling His purpose for your life.

Stay focused

Learn to write your goals. You can't just wish for things. You've got to take your pen and your paper out and write your goals and write your vision.

. . . Write the vision, and make it plain upon tables, that he may run that readeth it.

Habakkuk 2:2

One of the most important success skills that you must develop is the ability to stay focused. You can overcome any obstacle, or any adversity that might come your way, when you are a focused believer. Focused people are a threat to Satan's operations. The word *focus* is defined by *Webster's Dictionary* as ***the center of one's attention, that which has been resolved into a clear image.***

In order to be an excellent, superb, above average athlete, it demands focus. In order to become someone who is very successful in business, it demands focus. In order to obtain what God says is yours, you must be focused.

Passionate people and people who aspire to do great things are extremely focused. In other words, they have a clear image of what they desire in their lives. They see it every time they wake up. They see it throughout the day. They see it in their dreams. There is a clear image on the inside of them and it motivates them.

Focus requires a target. Without that target, you can't become focused. When you read God's Word and you discover God's promises for your life, then that creates a target.

. . . God shall supply all your need according to his riches in glory by Christ Jesus (Philippians 4:19) is designed by the Holy Ghost to become a target for your life.

If your needs are not met, if you're living in lack, if you're living from paycheck to paycheck, or if it seems that you always come up short, then you need to focus on that verse. That verse becomes your target.

I press toward the mark for the prize of the high calling of God in Christ Jesus.

Philippians 3:14

The Apostle Paul tells us to press toward the mark. That word ***press*** implies ***action, discipline, and an ongoing pursuit.*** That's where a lot of people miss out. They aren't willing to press and consequently they give up too quickly.

> ***Failure is just another way to more intelligently start over again. – Henry Ford***

Focused people are not easily distracted. Focused people refuse to compromise what they believe. They make no provision for failure. Focused people do not change what they believe because of circumstances. Focused people finish what they start. They will not give up. What is the "mark" you're pressing toward? Whatever it is, each day that you press toward it, you're getting a little closer.

I will cry to God Most High, Who performs on my behalf and rewards me [Who brings to pass His purposes for me and surely completes them]!

Psalm 57:2 (Amplified)

It's not enough to just be inspired. Inspiration is not enough. It's the starting point. But if God's Word is going to come to pass in your life then it requires sustained focus.

If you lose your focus, then you will be consumed with hopelessness. That's Satan's ultimate goal – to cause you to become hopeless.

The Spirit of God once said this to me, "For the believer, focus is determining where to direct your faith and holding it there until that which you are believing for comes to pass."

If it's healing that you need, then direct your faith to the healing scriptures. If it's financial deliverance that you need, then direct your faith toward the promises of God where finances are concerned. If it's the salvation of a loved one, then focus your faith on the promises of God and declare that you have a right to believe that your entire household will be saved. Don't give up until the manifestation comes to pass.

Avoid the focus-thieves

Life is full of distractions. It seems that every day either someone or something is trying to get us off track. I call them "focus-thieves." This is why we have to be on guard at all times.

Satan has many subtle ways of stealing our focus. One is by getting us to begin to murmur and complain because it seems that things are taking too long. Or he tries to get us upset because someone else got their breakthrough before we did.

This is why Paul stated that we must not be ignorant of Satan's devices (II Corinthians 2:11). When he has caused you to lose your focus, the result will be "wavering." You'll begin to doubt the validity of God's promise and your right for it to come to pass in your life.

Let us hold fast the profession of our faith without wavering; (for he is faithful that promised).

Hebrews 10:23

So let us seize and hold fast and retain . . .

Hebrews 10:23 (Amplified)

This gives the idea that our faith is trying to drift away but we must grasp it firmly and hold on to it with everything that is in us.

We can see how dangerous it is for us to allow ourselves to become distracted. Distractions not only steal our focus but also immobilize our faith.

. . . we have toiled all the night, and have taken nothing . . .

Luke 5:5

Many times we find ourselves in the same boat as Peter, doing everything we know to do yet at the end of the day we have nothing (in the natural) to show for it. We've prayed, we've confessed the Word, we've forgiven, and we've stood. We've renewed our mind, set our goals, watched our mouths – yet it looks as though nothing is working! It's Satan's attempt to get you to lose focus.

When it seems that nothing is happening, most people will become weary and discouraged and eventually give up. Obviously, this is exactly what Satan is hoping for. He wants to distract you when you are endeavoring to trust God.

The dictionary defines ***distraction*** as *a drawing apart or that which draws one in a different direction.*

Satan knows how dangerous a focused, single-minded Christian is to his operations. He knows that a focused, single-minded believer who is confident in who he is in Christ Jesus can obtain anything he dares to believe for. That's why he will do everything that he possibly can to draw this person in a different direction. He knows that a double-minded person can't receive anything from God (James 1:7-8).

Peter said that they had *"taken nothing"* but then he followed with these words; ***"... nevertheless at thy word ..."*** This is the most important thing that you can do when "nothing" is staring you in the face. By declaring this phrase, Peter kept himself from being pulled into a different direction. He overcame the distraction and later was rewarded in a big way.

Obviously as we discussed earlier, it takes discipline to stay focused on your goals. Discipline requires you to put the Word of God ahead of your **feelings** and your **emotions.** To lay hold upon that which the Word promises, you simply cannot rely on your feelings or your emotions. You have to stay focused on what you know is true from the Word of God.

Staying focused keeps you on the right path. Staying focused enables you to master and overcome every distraction. Staying focused helps you to get where you truly want to go.

Look out for the "focus-thieves" and keep your eyes fixed on God's promises and the goals He's given you to achieve.

Satan will try everything to get you to change your mind, doubt your ability to hear from God, and to back off from your commitment.

But thou hast fully known my doctrine, manner of life, <u>purpose</u>, faith, longsuffering, charity, patience, persecutions, afflictions, which came unto me at

Antioch, at Iconium, at Lystra; what persecutions I endured: but out of them all the Lord delivered me. Yea, and all that will live godly in Christ Jesus shall suffer persecution. But evil men and seducers shall wax worse, deceiving, and being deceived. But continue thou in the things which thou hast learned and hast been assured of, knowing of whom thou hast learned them.

II Timothy 3:10-14

In these passages, God is saying that even though everything seems to be getting worse, we are to continue in the things which we have learned. No matter how our situation may appear, we are to remember that nothing can separate us from the love of Christ. Despite the difficult circumstances in which we may find ourselves, or the doubt Satan tries to put in our minds, we are not to back away from our commitment. Solomon tells us:

When you make a vow to God, do not delay in fulfilling it. He has no pleasure in fools; fulfill your vow. It is better not to vow than to make a vow and not fulfill it.

Ecclesiastes 5:4-5 (NIV)

When you fall, get up and start over again

Remember, it is not over because you've fallen or been knocked down. It is not over because you made a mistake.

. . . when I fall, I shall arise . . .

Micah 7:8

The most natural thing for you to do when you fall is to get up. It is not natural to stay down. It is not natural to just lay there for the rest of your life.

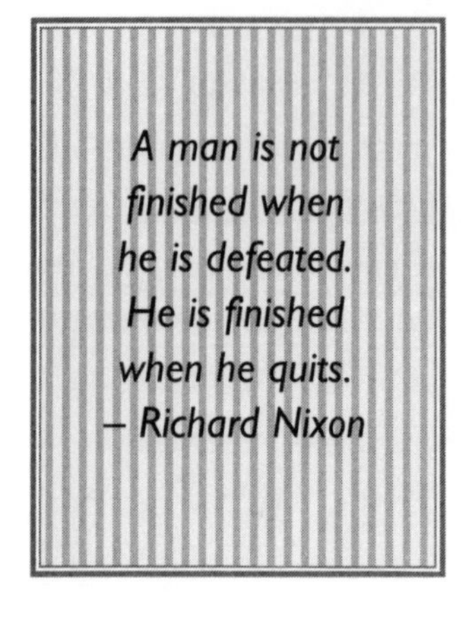

What would you think of me if I fell off a platform while preaching and landed on my back on the floor? Somebody rushes up and says, *"Jerry, are you okay? Are you hurt?"* I move around and check myself out and say, "No, I think I am okay."

"Well, can we help you up?"

"No, oh no, you don't understand. I fell."

"Well, yes Jerry, we saw you fall but you said you are okay so can we help you up?"

"No, no, it may be God's will that I be down here."

"Jerry, it couldn't be God's will. It was God's will for you to be on the platform and not fall on the floor."

"Yes, but God may be teaching me something while I am down here."

That is stupid.

Yet there are a lot of Christians who live that way. They make a mistake. They fall, and refuse to get up, and they live in the past for the rest of their lives.

If I stumble and fall off a platform, you better believe that I am going to get up. I am going to get up so quick and hope to God that no one saw me fall. I have had it happen before! It was very embarrassing.

When I first started in the ministry, I was preaching on a platform that was about twelve feet long and about two feet wide. Back then I just ran from one end of the platform to the other. I preached as fast as I could because I didn't know if they would ask me back and I wanted to tell them everything I knew. So I was running and preaching and I got too close to the edge. All the musical instruments were on the main floor. I fell off the back of the platform and landed in the base drum. My bottom was in the base drum. My arms and legs were sticking out of that base drum. Everybody got up to see where I went. I was thinking, *God, I can't believe I fell off the platform.*

I asked God, "What do I do now?"

He said, "Get up. Do a Micah 7:8 and do it quick, boy."

I asked, "What is Micah 7:8?"

He said, "It says, When I fall I shall arise. Now don't ask any more questions, boy. Get up and do it quickly."

I asked, "What do I tell the people?" He said, "Don't even mention the fall. Take up where you left off."

I got out of that base drum, got myself back up on that platform, and just kept preaching. I didn't even mention falling. I just acted like that was the way I preached all the time.

But after the service somebody came up to me (there is always one in every crowd), *"Jerry Savelle, why did you fall?"*

I said, "It was an accident."

"Have you got a problem? Do you fall often?"

"No maam, I don't fall often. It was an accident. Let's not talk about the fall. Did you see that recovery? Wasn't that a great recovery?"

"I have never seen a preacher fall off the platform."

I said, "Let's not talk about the fall, let's talk about the recovery."

However, I could not get this person to stop talking about the fall, so I finally just walked away.

Don't allow the devil to keep you down. Don't allow him to control you by fear. It is time to get up and brush yourself off and start moving into what God wants to do with your life.

In other words, stop talking about your past mistakes, your past failures, the "old" you . . . and start focusing on your recovery. It's a new day in your life.

God is saying that He needs you, and He wants you, He has put something so special and so unique on the inside of you that will be a "hope" and a testimony to others.

Don't let your life just go by without discovering why you were put on this earth. God had a purpose for creating you. Nothing He does is by accident.

I encourage you to go over each chapter in this book until you believe what His Word says about you. Confess His Word about you until your image of yourself is transformed into the image of God. Embrace the qualities and personality traits He's given you and use them in a positive way. Stop focusing on the negative things about yourself.

Look at your life as a story and a message that will help someone else. There is only one just like you. Be free to be yourself.